Teacher Preparation Classroom

TEACHER PREP

MERRILL
PRENTICE HALL

See a demo at
www.prenhall.com/teacherprep/demo

Your Class. Their Careers. Our Future. Will your students be prepared?

We invite you to explore our new, innovative and engaging website and all that it has to offer you, your course, and tomorrow's educators! Preview this site today at www.prenhall.com/teacherprep/demo. Just click on "go" on the login page to begin your exploration.

Organized around the major courses pre-service teachers take, the Teacher Preparation site provides media, student/teacher artifacts, strategies, research articles, and other resources to equip your students with the quality tools needed to excel in their courses and prepare them for their first classroom.

This ultimate online education resource will provide you and your students access to:

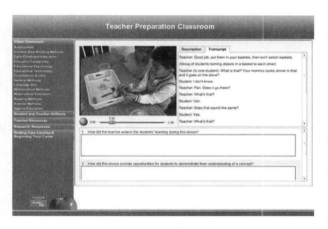

Online Video Library. More than 250 video clips—each tied to a course topic and framed by learning goals and Praxis-type questions—capture real teachers and students working in real classrooms.

Student and Teacher Artifacts. More than 200 student and teacher classroom artifacts—each tied to a course topic and framed by learning goals and application questions—provide a wealth of materials and experiences to help your students observe children's developmental learning.

Lesson Plan Builder. Step-by-step guidelines and lesson plan examples support students as they learn to build high-quality lesson plans.

Articles and Readings. Over 500 articles from ASCD's renowned journal *Educational Leadership* are available. The site also includes Research Navigator, a searchable database of additional educational journals.

Strategy and Lessons. Over 500 research-supported instructional strategies appropriate for a wide range of grade levels and content areas.

Licensure and Career Tools. Resources devoted to helping your students pass their licensure exam; learn standards, law and public policies; plan a teaching portfolio; and succeed in their first year of teaching.

How to ORDER *Teacher Prep* for you and your students:

For students to receive a *Teacher Prep* Access Code with this text, instructors **must** provide a special value pack ISBN number on their textbook order form. To receive this special ISBN, please email: Merrill.marketing@pearsoned.com and provide the following information:

- Name and Affiliation
- Author/Title/Edition of Merrill text

Upon ordering Teacher Prep for their students, instructors will be given a lifetime Teacher Prep Access Code.

A Practical Guide for Special Education Professionals

Lisa R. Churchill

California State University, Chico

Rita Mulholland

Richard Stockton College

Michelle R. Cepello

California State University, Chico

PEARSON

Merrill
Prentice Hall

Upper Saddle River, New Jersey
Columbus, Ohio

Library of Congress Cataloging in Publication Data

Churchill, Lisa.
   A practical guide for special education professionals/authors: Lisa R. Churchill, Rita Mulholland, Michelle R. Cepello.
     p.cm.
   Includes bibliographical references and index.
   ISBN–13: 978-0-13-172021-3
   1. Special education—United States. 2. Individualized education programs—United States. I. Mulholland, Rita. II. Cepello, Michelle R. III. Title.
LC3981.C5 2008
371.90973—dc22

2007032421

Vice President and Executive Publisher: Jeffery W. Johnston
Executive Editor: Ann Castel Davis
Editorial Assistant: Penny Burleson
Production Editor: Sheryl Glicker Langner
Production Coordination: Mary Tindle, S4Carlisle Publishing Services
Photo Coordinator: Maria B. Vonada
Design Coordinator: Diane C. Lorenzo
Cover Design: Aaron Dixon
Cover Image: Fotosearch
Production Manager: Laura Messerly
Director of Marketing: David Gesell
Marketing Manager: Autumn Purdy
Marketing Coordinator: Brian Mounts

This book was set in Garamond by S4Carlisle Publishing Services. It was printed and bound by Bind Rite, Inc. The cover was printed by Phoenix Color Corp.

Chapter Opener Photo Credits: Lori Whitley/Merrill, Chapters 1 and 2; Valerie Schultz/Merrill, Chapter 3; Liz Moore/Merrill, Chapter 4; Krista Greco/Merrill, Chapters 5, 6, 9, and 10; David Mager/Pearson Learning Photo Studio, Chapter 7; Anne Vega/Merrill, Chapter 8; Michael Littlejohn/PH College, Chapter 11.

Pearson Education Ltd.
Pearson Education Singapore Pte. Ltd.
Pearson Education Canada, Ltd.
Pearson Education–Japan

Pearson Education Australia Pty. Limited
Pearson Education North Asia Ltd.
Pearson Educación de Mexico, S.A. de C.V.
Pearson Education Malaysia Pte. Ltd.

10 9 8 7 6 5 4 3 2 1
ISBN-13: 978-0-13-172021-3
ISBN-10:   0-13-172021-X

ABOUT THE AUTHORS

Lisa R. Churchill, PhD, is a Professor of Special Education at California State University, Chico in the Professional Studies in Education Department. She taught special education for 14 years for the public schools, in multiple settings ranging from a large comprehensive urban high school to a small rural country school, residential programs, and mental health hospitals. Her teaching experience spans pre-school to adult education. At Chico State, Dr. Churchill served as the Education Specialist Internship Program Director, Project Director for numerous federal Office of Special Education Programs (OSEP) grants, and coordinator for the Masters in Special Education program. She was instrumental in designing and writing the University's Education Specialist Level II program that focuses on induction, mentoring, and support for the beginning special education professional. Her presentations and publications focus on alternative certification issues and highlight the "Northeastern California Partnership for Special Education," an award-winning program recognized as the 2004 Exemplary Teacher Preparation Program by the American Council on Rural Special Education (ACRES) and as a "model site" by the U.S.D.O.E. Office of Innovation and Improvement. Dr. Churchill was the recipient of the California State University, Chico Professional Achievement Honor for excellence in teaching and significant contributions to her discipline in 2006.

Rita Mulholland, PhD, is an Assistant Professor at Richard Stockton College (NJ) in the Teacher Education/Special Education Program. She taught for 25 years at the elementary, middle, and secondary levels as a general educator, reading specialist, and special educator. Her publications and conference presentations address supporting struggling learners. Dr. Mulholland works as a consultant with the IRA and US AID in Macedonia to support teachers in improving the classroom learning environment. She was the recipient of a Fulbright-Hays grant to work with university colleagues in South Africa. Her research interest is in the area of incorporating technology into teaching.

Michelle Cepello, EdD, comes to the field of education with over 20 years of experience working as a general and special education teacher, program specialist, and university professor. She currently serves as the Program Coordinator for the Education Specialist Credential Program at California State University, Chico and teaches courses on collaboration, consultation, staff development and special education curriculum and instruction. Dr. Cepello has had the honor of working closely with regional partners in the implementation of several federal grants that promote the recruitment, professional preparation, and retention of special education teachers. Her research focus is in the areas of service learning methodology for individuals with moderate/severe needs and alternative certification programs.

PREFACE

RATIONALE

A Practical Guide for Special Education Professionals is a resource guidebook designed especially for students who are taking a course where time will be spent in observing or teaching in a field-based setting. This guide is also applicable for beginning special educators, as well as teachers who are enrolled in Alternative Certification Programs and are earning their credentials while simultaneously working in the classroom as instructors of record. The purpose of this guidebook is to provide practical information and suggestions to help the special education teacher candidate or the beginning special educator survive and eventually succeed in the school and classroom setting. *A Practical Guide for Special Education Professionals* is written to be used as a quick reference. Thus, the chapters are presented in a brief, user-friendly format. The guidebook's content presents an overview of the major elements of teaching special education.

We believe that it is important for all special educators to have an overview or "big picture" of the major elements in the field. Thus, we selected topics that are deemed essential and that can be readily applied to the classroom. This guidebook is to act as a "survival guide" for special educators, and as a resource to support and benefit students and beginning special education teachers. Each chapter of this book prepares the teacher to work effectively in special education by supplying strategies and practical tips for working directly with pupils as well as other adults in the educational setting.

Content topics include: special education overview, the individualized education program (IEP), classroom and individual behavior management, assessment for instruction, instructional planning and strategies, supervision of paraprofessionals, collaborative consultation, home/school partnerships, stress reduction strategies, and time management techniques. Overall, the content is applicable to teachers serving students with disabilities, although there is content more specific to students with mild to moderate disabilities in Chapter 6, Instructional Planning, and Chapter 7, Instructional Strategies.

ORGANIZATION OF THE TEXT

Application in the field determined the organization of the chapters. From our experiences as classroom teachers and university supervisors, we know that beginning special education teachers "need it all," and the sooner the better. Thus, we have designed the text so that the material presented in each chapter is readily accessible, and does not rely on information contained in a previous chapter. Chapter 1 provides an introduction to the special education profession by presenting the federal definition of special education, a brief historical background on special education legislation, and a list of special education terms and acronyms. A description of the roles and dispositions of special educators is also included. Chapter 2 discusses IEP legal and pragmatic issues. We consider the IEP the "heart" of special education, and so placed this content at the beginning of the text. Chapter 3 presents practical tips for managing the classroom, such as recommendations for rules and procedures, steps for reducing classroom disruptions, suggestions for implementing a classroom reward system, and guidelines for conducting class meetings. Chapter 4 focuses on individual behavior management and positive behavioral supports. Chapter 5 reviews assessment for instruction and highlights responsiveness to intervention (RTI). Chapters 6 and 7 provide practical tips for instructional planning and strategies. Chapter 6, Instructional Planning, includes sections on using mnemonics, universal design, assistive technology, grading software, and academic learning time (ALT). Chapter 7 focuses on instructional strategies that are most commonly used by special educators and briefly reviews explicit instruction, concept development teaching, cooperative learning, reciprocal teaching, and service learning. Both Chapters 6 and 7 reference invaluable resources on the Internet and in the literature that students can use to further enhance their professional skills and improve their classroom practice. Chapter 8, Supervision of Paraprofessionals, deals with an area of concern for most beginning special educators. Strategies for promoting positive working relationships with paraprofessionals are outlined in this chapter. Chapter 9 examines the role of the special education teacher as a collaborative consultant. Guidelines and forms are provided to foster positive communication between general education teachers and the special educator. Chapter 10 continues to offer recommendations for establishing home and school partnerships that value family members and legal guardians as active participants in the educational programs of students with disabilities. Chapter 11 addresses the "overwhelmed" feeling that most special educators experience as they enter the profession. The first year of teaching and the reality of the teaching responsibilities in and out of the classroom require multitasking skills. To assist the beginning professional in moving from "survival" to "success," stress reduction and time management strategies are presented. Professional organizations and resources to sustain professional growth and development are also included.

FEATURES OF THE TEXT

Chapter features include:

- *Objectives:* At the beginning of each chapter, objectives highlight the chapter's purpose and guide the reader to focus on the main points.
- *Presentation of Information:* The text is written in a user-friendly format that is clear and concise. Figures are used to summarize and underscore information.

- *Teaching Tips and Forms:* Most chapters include practical tips and forms that apply to the daily activities of the special educator.
- *Quotations:* Motivational quotations are included in each chapter to enhance the presentation of the material.
- *Take a Moment:* This activity for reflection is included to encourage readers to think, reflect, and respond to questions related to specific content throughout each chapter.
- *Did You Know?* Information in this feature summarizes interesting facts and figures related to the chapter's topic.
- *Explorations:* These exercises at the conclusion of each chapter assist the reader in applying the chapter content to his or her specific teaching situation.
- *Web Sites:* Chapter Listings of Internet Resources provide quick references to help students further explore chapter content and connect to the most recent information on related topics.
- *References*: References and resources related to the chapter's content are listed at the end of each chapter to encourage further research.

ACKNOWLEDGMENTS

We wish to express our appreciation to the many individuals who have contributed to the creation and production of this book. Our inspiration stems from many years of working with highly dedicated students, teachers, professors, and administrators. We have been very grateful for the continuous support and professional encouragement of our fellow colleagues at Chico State: Dr. Mary Jensen, Dr. Terri Davis, Dr. Jim Richmond, Mr. Vern Milliken, Ms. Laurel Hill-Ward, Ms. Julie Dahl, Ms. Denise Dion, Ms. Cheri Taylor, Dr. Cindy Ratekin, Dr. Hsuying Ward, Ms. Gloria Prochaska, Ms. Emily Davis, Ms. Cherie Evanhoe, Ms. Vicky Shadd, Mr. Jack Krause, Dr. Mike Carroll, Dr. Steven Koch, Ms. Linda Carol, Ms. Glenda Anderson, and Mr. Tom Neeley. It is clear to us that it really does take a "team" to certify a teacher candidate.

Numerous individuals at Merrill/Prentice Hall generously provided support for this project. We would like to acknowledge and thank them for their efforts: Ann Davis, Executive Editor; Penny Burleson, Editorial Assistant; and Sheryl Langner, Production Editor. We would also like to thank all the reviewers: Fran Butler, Weber State University; Doug Feldmann, Northern Kentucky University; Michele Wilson Kamens, Rider University; Mary Provost, College of Charleston; Laura Reissner, Northern Michigan University; Lech Wisniewski, Metropolitan State College of Denver; Carmel Collum Yarger, Utah State University; and Linda Young, Indiana University, South Bend.

Many contributors offered input for this book. We greatly appreciate their research, ideas, and practical applications, as well as the privilege to publish their material within the pages of this text.

We would like to acknowledge our families and friends who understood our need for time away from them to complete this project, and thank them for their patience and understanding.

Finally, we would like to acknowledge all the individuals who have decided to become special educators and those who have dedicated their lives' work to teaching individuals with exceptional needs. You are our inspiration for a better, peaceful world. We dedicate this book to special educators and their efforts to make a difference in the lives of others.

DISCOVER THE MERRILL RESOURCES FOR SPECIAL EDUCATION WEBSITE

Technology is a constantly growing and changing aspect of our field that is creating a need for new content and resources. To address this emerging need, Merrill Education has developed an online learning environment for students, teachers, and professors alike to complement our products—the *Merrill Resources for Special Education* Website. This content-rich website provides additional resources specific to this book's topic and will help you—professors, classroom teachers, and students—augment your teaching, learning, and professional development.

Our goal is to build on and enhance what our products already offer. For this reason, the content for our user-friendly website is organized by topic and provides teachers, professors, and students with a variety of meaningful resources all in one location. With this website, we bring together the best of what Merrill has to offer: text resources, video clips, web links, tutorials, and a wide variety of information on topics of interest to general and special educators alike. Rich content, applications, and competencies further enhance the learning process.

The *Merrill Resources for Special Education* Website includes:

- Video clips specific to each topic, with questions to help you evaluate the content and make crucial theory-to-practice connections.
- Thought-provoking critical analysis questions that students can answer and turn in for evaluation or that can serve as basis for class discussions and lectures.
- Access to a wide variety of resources related to classroom strategies and methods, including lesson planning and classroom management.
- Information on all the most current relevant topics related to special and general education, including CEC and Praxis™ standards, IEPs, portfolios, and professional development.
- Extensive web resources and overviews on each topic addressed on the website.
- A search feature to help access specific information quickly.

To take advantage of these and other resources, please visit the *Merrill Resources for Special Education* Website at

http://www.prenhall.com/churchill

BRIEF CONTENTS

CONTENTS

CHAPTER 3

CLASSROOM MANAGEMENT AND ORGANIZATION   46

CHAPTER 10

HOME–SCHOOL PARTNERSHIPS   152

CHAPTER 11

SURVIVAL TO SUCCESS: STRESS REDUCTION AND TIME MANAGEMENT STRATEGIES   168

Note: Every effort has been made to provide accurate and current Internet information in this book. However, the Internet and information posted on it are constantly changing, and it is inevitable that some of the Internet addresses listed in this textbook will change.

1

An Overview of Special Education

"The function of education is to teach one to think intensively and to think critically. . . . Intelligence plus character—that is the goal of education."

Martin Luther King, Jr.

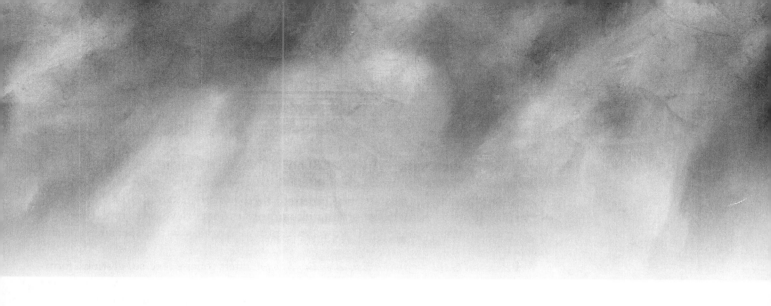

CHAPTER OBJECTIVES

■ Introduce guidebook contents and key features
■ Review federal definition of special education
■ Provide historical background on special education
■ Discuss the roles of the special educator
■ Review special education terms and acronyms

Before reading this chapter, take a moment to note what comes to mind when you think of special education. Do you know the federal definition of special education? How familiar are you with special education terminology? Why do you want to work in the special education profession? Record your reflections and revisit your response as you read this chapter.

INTRODUCTION

This guidebook is designed for individuals who are observing or teaching in a field-based setting, teachers enrolled in an alternative certification preparation program that includes an on-the-job training component or internship, as well as the beginning special educator who has completed certification and now faces the realities of his or her own classroom setting. Written from a practical perspective, this text provides the reader needed resources to address legal issues, instructional and behavioral strategies, assessment for instruction, as well as tips for working with families, supervising paraprofessionals, and collaborating with general education teachers. Special educators need this information to successfully participate in the development and implementation of individualized education programs (IEPs) for their pupils with disabilities. This guidebook is to be used as a quick reference, so chapters are brief and user-friendly.

The rationale for writing this guidebook stems from practical need. Special education teachers' needs are intense and extensive. Special educators are immediately faced with legal and organizational issues as soon as they step into the classroom.

In this book you will learn about the foundations of special education, classroom management and organization, stress reduction and time management strategies, and practical approaches to improving communications with other teachers and parents. Descriptions of special education service delivery models; a guide to terms, definitions, and acronyms used in the special education field; and details of the individualized education program (IEP) process and document that highlight legal and pragmatic issues are also featured. Additionally, examples of time-saving forms, applicable instructional strategies, and professional development activities to sustain continuous professional growth are provided to assist the special education teacher.

A Practical Guide for Special Education Professionals offers concise text, suggestions, forms, and tips for the new special education professional to begin his or her teaching career. Chapters are short and the content is directly applicable to the classroom. Each chapter provides objectives to focus the reader and closing activities that reinforce the chapter's content. A major strength of this book is that it addresses the critical issues, content, and pedagogy needed by today's special education professional and applies directly to the daily activities of the teacher.

To introduce you to the special education profession, we begin by reviewing the federal definition of special education and provide a brief historical overview of the legislation that supports its implementation. The multiple roles of the special education teacher are also described to help you understand where special education services are delivered and what it means to be a special educator in today's classrooms.

Being familiar with the language of special education, especially its extensive alphabet soup of acronyms, helps to demystify the profession. Thus, we have included in this chapter a list of acronyms commonly used in special education. Although these terms may vary from state to state, we have included the terms that are generally used in the literature and in the field to provide a quick reference for you.

FEDERAL DEFINITION OF SPECIAL EDUCATION

The law defines special education as "specially designed instruction" to meet the individual needs of an exceptional child. Special education refers to the educational program designed for students with exceptionalities who may need instructional accommodations (in classrooms, hospitals, institutions, or the home), curricular adaptations, and/or related services to be successful in school and prepared for either further education or the workforce. Terms defining various exceptionalities have changed over the years and new terms have been included in the law. Exceptionalities include learners with:

- Mental retardation
- Learning disabilities
- Attention deficit hyperactive disorders
- Communication disorders
- Emotional disorders
- Blindness or low vision
- Physical disabilities or other health impairments
- Deaf or hard-of-hearing issues
- Multiple and severe disabilities

It is important to know and understand the characteristics of each exceptionality when planning an instructional program to meet the needs of all your students. We suggest that you visit the Websites listed at the end of this chapter for more specific information on each category. A particularly useful Website for descriptions of disabilities is the National Dissemination Center for Children with Disabilities at http://www.nichcy.org/disabinf.asp.

HISTORICAL BACKGROUND ON SPECIAL EDUCATION

In the 1800s the federal government provided grants to states to educate children who were visually impaired and deaf. Throughout the first half of the 20th century, the federal government had little involvement in public schools.

Over 30 years later in 1954 with the *Brown vs. Board of Education* decision, children with exceptionalities were guaranteed the right to an equal education, but many special needs students still did not receive services. Advocates for individuals with exceptionalities, including parents, teachers, and representatives from national organizations, continued to promote the need for new legislation that would identify the rights of all students with exceptionalities.

In the 1960s the Elementary and Secondary Education Act, which ensures the federal government's support for public schools, was passed. This same act was amended to include federal support to state schools that educated children with exceptionalities. In 1966, the Bureau for the Education of the Handicapped (BEH) was created to provide grants to states to improve their education programs for students with disabilities. This agency recommended the creation of one program to solidify all the efforts in supporting special education services.

In 1975, Congress passed the Education for All Handicapped Children Act (PL 94–142), which was the first federal legislation to identify the rights of children with exceptionalities from 3 to 21 years of age. The law specified that students with special needs were entitled to a free and appropriate public education (FAPE) in the least restrictive environment (LRE). As members of the student's educational team, parents were afforded due process rights and students were entitled to a written individualized education program (IEP), which is developed by a team comprised of all those involved in the education of the student (see Chapter 2 for historical, practical, and legal issues regarding IEPs).

Over the next 15 years, several amendments were made to this law that addressed funding (PL 98–199 authorizing funding for parent training to protect the rights of a child), early intervention (PL 99–457 mandating services from birth), assistive technology (PL 100–407 authorizing funding for technological assistance), and vocational education (PL 101–392 requiring access to vocational programs).

The Individuals with Disabilities Education Act, or IDEA, was enacted in 1994 and then amended in 1997 and reauthorized in 2004. Details of the 2004 IDEA legislation are highlighted in Chapter 2.

The field of special education has evolved over time. From its legal beginnings, influenced by the civil rights movement, a major part of special education advocacy has been to provide free appropriate public education (FAPE) to students with disabilities in the least restrictive environment (LRE).

MULTIPLE ROLES OF THE SPECIAL EDUCATOR

According to the National Personnel Center for Special Education Personnel and Related Service Providers Website (http://www.personnelcenter.org), special educators are: "creative problem solvers; capable of understanding a variety of learning styles and teaching strategies; care about the future of infants, young children and youth with disabilities and their families; team players; intelligent, organized and flexible; lifelong learners; and prepared to meet the challenges of their profession with confidence and enthusiasm."

Special educators have many roles that can change daily depending on what needs to be accomplished. In addition to the traditional role of teacher, a special educator is also a skilled diagnostician, an organized case manager, an articulate advocate, a collaborative consultant, and a staff developer. A special educator has the responsibility to assess how each student learns and to design or modify instruction that results in positive educational outcomes regardless of where the special education services are provided. Special educators may work in public and private schools, residential facilities, hospitals or clinics, and sometimes in the student's home.

Special educators work very closely with colleagues, administrators, students, and family members of their students. What happens in and out of the classroom determines how successful you will be in your new profession. Special education teaching can be challenging. In addition to providing instruction, the special educator must also assess student learning, modify curriculum, write IEP goals, monitor IEP goals and special education services, report student progress to parents, plan and collaborate with other teachers, supervise paraprofessionals, resolve scheduling conflicts, counsel students, attend IEP meetings, and communicate with administrators and psychologists on a regular basis. Clear and frequent communication is a key to success as a special educator.

SPECIAL EDUCATION TERMINOLOGY

Special education laws and practice have created a professional language that can be difficult to navigate through at times. We have included a resource section with frequently used special education acronyms at the end of this chapter to help you understand these terms and provide a quick reference. Figure 1.1 asks you to reflect on legal and professional aspects of special education.

FIGURE 1.1

Take a Moment

Think About	Reflect	Respond
Federal definition of special education	What are the key points to remember about this definition?	
Special education terminology	What terms or acronyms are not familiar to you?	
	What strategy will you use to find out what they mean?	
Being a special educator	What characteristics and attributes do you possess that will help you to be a successful special educator?	

CONCLUSION

Special education law continues to evolve. Recognition of disabilities not previously identified may be added, and changes in legal timelines, placement issues, assessments, technology updates, and so on may be addressed. Interpretations and issues continue to be clarified through hearings and the courts.

The role of the special educator is also evolving. However, one notion is clear. Although special educators have multiple roles, a common reason why individuals enter this field is because they have a great desire to make a difference in the lives of students with disabilities and their families.

EXPLORATIONS

1. Review the federal definition of special education. Survey the general education teachers, paraprofessionals, and administrators at your site to see if they know this definition. In the process of surveying them, use this opportunity to share information about this definition.
2. Many acronyms are used in special education. Parents, general education teachers, and administrators may not be familiar with some of these acronyms. What can you do to help others at your school site understand special education terminology and acronyms?
3. Special education teaching can be challenging. Clear and frequent communication is a key to success as a special educator. Develop a plan for communicating with others by writing three ways you plan to communicate with parents, other teachers, paraprofessionals, your site administrator, and your students.
4. Think about why you want to be a special educator. Write down your response and post it near your desk as a gentle motivator.

WEBSITES

Center for Applied Special Technology (CAST)
http://cast.org
This site provides technology-based educational resources and strategies.

Council for Exceptional Children's Summary of Significant Issues in IDEA 2004
http://www.cec.sped.org/pp/IDEA_120204.pdf
This site summarizes the significant issues of IDEA 2004.

IDEA 2004 (PL 108-446)
http://www.copyright.gov/legislation/p1108-446.html#306
This site has the IDEA 2004 document.

Massachusetts Department of Education
http://www.doe.mass.edu/sped/definitions.html
This site offers disability definitions and related links.

National Association of School Psychologists
http://www.nasponline.org/advocacy/IDEAinformation.html
This site provides information on public policy and legislative issues.

National Center for Special Education Personnel and Related Service Providers
http://www.personnelcenter.org
This site offers information on becoming a special educator and resources for recruiting, preparing, and retaining special educators.

National Center for the Dissemination of Disability Research
http://www.ncddr.org/
This site offers research, technical assistance, and demonstration activities focusing on the dissemination and utilization of disability research.

National Dissemination Center for Children with Disabilities
http://www.nichcy.org/
This site is a central source of information on disabilities, IDEA, No Child Left Behind, and research-based information on effective educational practices.

No Child Left Behind (NCLB), PL 107–110
http://www.wrightslaw.com/nclb/law/nclb.107-110.pdf
This site provides the full text of the law as introduced in 2001.

PE Central
http://www.pecentral.org/adapted/adapteddisabilities.html
This site defines and describes common disabilities and links to valuable resources.

Special Education Resources on the Internet
http://seriweb.com
This site links to many Internet sites related to students who have disabilities.

Teach California Website
http://teachcalifornia.org
This site offers background information on becoming a special educator and promotes special education personnel recruitment.

U.S. House of Representatives Report 108-77
http://www.nasponline.org/advocacy/IDEAHouseReport.pdf
This site features the report of the House of Representatives on IDEA.

U.S. Senate Report 108-105
http://edworkforce.house.gov/issues/108th/education/idea/conferencereport/confrept.htm
This site features the committee's report on IDEA.

Wrights Law
http://www.wrightslaw.com/
This site provides reliable information about special education law and advocacy for children with disabilities.

REFERENCES

Daugherty, R. (2001). *Special education: A summary of legal requirements, terms, and trends.* Westport, CT: Bergin & Garvey.

Education for All Handicapped Children Act of 1975, PL 94–142. Washington, DC: U.S. Department of Education.

Individuals with Disabilities Education Act (IDEA) of 1997, PL 105–17. Washington, DC: U.S. Department of Education.

Individuals with Disabilities Education Improvement Act of 2004, PL 108–446. Washington, DC: U.S. Department of Education.

Kauffman, J., & Hallahan, D. (2005). *Special education: What it is and why we need it.* Boston, MA: Allyn & Bacon.

Kirk, S., Gallagher, J., Anastasiow, N., & Coleman, M. (2006). *Educating exceptional children.* Boston, MA: Houghton Mifflin.

Mandlawitz, M. (2006). *What every teacher should know about IDEA 2004.* Boston, MA: Allyn & Bacon.

National Information Center for Children and Youth with Disabilities (NICHCY). (2001). *General information about disabilities.* Washington, DC: Author.

National Research Council. (2002). *Minority students in special and gifted education.* Washington, DC: National Academy Press.

Orelove, R., Sobrey, D., & Silberman, R. (2004). *Educating children with multiple disabilities* (4th ed). Baltimore, MD: Brookes.

Salend, S., & Salinas, A. (2003). Language differences or learning difficulties. *Teaching Exceptional Children*, 35(4), 36–43.

Smith, D. (2004). *Introduction to special education.* Boston, MA: Allyn & Bacon.

Sorrells, A., Rieth, H., & Sindelar, P. (Eds.). (2004). *Critical issues in special education.* Boston, MA: Allyn & Bacon.

Timmer, S. (2005). *Pigeonholes are for pigeons.* Joliet, IL: Premier Publications.

U.S. Department of Education. (2003). *Twenty-fourth annual report to Congress on implementation of the Individuals with Disabilities Education Act.* Washington, DC: Author.

Vaughn, S., Box, C., & Schumm, J. (2003). *Teaching exceptional, diverse, and at-risk students.* Boston, MA: Allyn & Bacon.

RESOURCES

SPECIAL EDUCATION TERMS

Source: Terms adapted from ERIC EC Digest No. #E560 (*http://ericec.org/digests/e560.html*).

Autism: A developmental disability significantly affecting verbal and nonverbal communication and social interaction, generally evident before age 3, that adversely affects a child's educational performance. Other characteristics often associated with autism are engagement in repetitive activities and stereotyped movements, resistance to environmental change or change in daily routines, and unusual responses to sensory experiences. The term does not apply if a child's educational performance is adversely affected primarily because the child has a serious emotional disturbance as defined herein.

Deaf-blindness: A combination of hearing and visual impairments causing such severe communication, developmental, and educational problems that the student cannot be accommodated in either a program specifically for the deaf or a program specifically for the blind.

Deafness: A hearing loss severe enough that the student cannot understand what is being said even with a hearing aid.

Emotional disturbance: A condition exhibiting one or more of the following characteristics, displayed over a long period of time and to a marked degree, that adversely affects a child's educational performance:

> An inability to learn that cannot be explained by intellectual, sensory, or health factors
>
> An inability to build or maintain satisfactory interpersonal relationships with peers or teachers
>
> Inappropriate types of behavior or feelings under normal circumstances
>
> A general pervasive mood of unhappiness or depression
>
> A tendency to develop physical symptoms or fears associated with personal or school problems

This term includes schizophrenia, but does not include students who are socially maladjusted, unless they have an emotional disturbance.

Hard of hearing: An impairment in hearing, whether permanent or fluctuating, that adversely affects a student's educational performance but is not included under the definition of deafness as listed herein.

Learning disability: A disorder in one or more of the basic psychological processes involved in understanding or in using language, spoken or written, that may manifest itself in an imperfect ability to listen, think, speak, read, write, spell, or do mathematical calculations. This term includes such conditions as perceptual disabilities, brain injury, minimal brain dysfunction, dyslexia, and developmental aphasia. This term does not include children who have learning problems that are primarily the result of visual, hearing, or motor disabilities; mental retardation; or environmental, cultural, or economic disadvantage.

Mental retardation: Significantly subaverage general intellectual functioning, existing concurrently with deficits in adaptive behavior and manifested during the developmental period, that adversely affects a child's educational performance.

Multiple disabilities: A combination of impairments (such as mental retardation and blindness, or mental retardation and physical disabilities) that causes such severe educational problems that the child cannot be accommodated in a special education program solely for one of the impairments. The term does not include deaf-blindness.

Orthopedic impairment: A severe orthopedic impairment that adversely affects educational performance. The term includes impairments such as amputation, absence of a limb, cerebral palsy, poliomyelitis, and bone tuberculosis.

Other health impairment: Having limited strength, vitality, or alertness due to chronic or acute health problems, such as a heart condition, rheumatic fever, asthma, hemophilia, and leukemia, that adversely affect educational performance.

Speech or language impairment: A communication disorder such as stuttering, impaired articulation, language impairment, or a voice impairment that adversely affects a student's educational performance but is not related to hearing loss.

Traumatic brain injury: An acquired injury to the brain caused by an external physical force, resulting in total or partial functional disability or psychosocial impairment, or both, that adversely affects a child's educational performance. The term applies to open or closed head injuries resulting in impairments in one or more areas, such as cognition; language; memory; attention; reasoning; abstract thinking; judgment; problem-solving; sensory, perceptual, and motor abilities; psychosocial behavior; physical functions; information processing; and speech. The term does not apply to brain injuries that are congenital or degenerative, or brain injuries induced by birth trauma.

Visual impairment, including blindness: An impairment in vision that, even with correction, adversely affects a child's educational performance. The term includes both partial sight and blindness.

DEFINITIONS OF RELATED SERVICES

Adapted from U.S. Department of Education, Office of Special Education Programs' (OSEP's) IDEA website *(http://idea.ed.gov/explore/home)*.

The **IDEA Regulations** define related services as:

(a) General. Related services means transportation and such developmental, corrective, and other supportive services as are required to assist a child with a disability to benefit from special education, and includes speech-language pathology and audiology services, interpreting services, psychological services, physical and occupational therapy, recreation, including therapeutic recreation, early identification and assessment of disabilities in children, counseling services, including rehabilitation counseling, orientation and mobility services, and medical services for diagnostic or evaluation purposes. Related services also include school health services and school nurse services, social work services in schools, and parent counseling and training.

(b) Exception; services that apply to children with surgically implanted devices, including cochlear implants.

(1) Related services do not include a medical device that is surgically implanted, the optimization of that device's functioning (e.g., mapping), maintenance of that device, or the replacement of that device.

(2) Nothing in paragraph (b)(1) of this section—
(i) Limits the right of a child with a surgically implanted device (e.g., cochlear implant) to receive related services (as listed in paragraph (a) of this section) that are determined by the IEP Team to be necessary for the child to receive FAPE.
(ii) Limits the responsibility of a public agency to appropriately monitor and maintain medical devices that are needed to maintain the health and safety of the child, including breathing, nutrition, or operation of other bodily functions, while the child is transported to and from school or is at school; or
(iii) Prevents the routine checking of an external component of a surgically-implanted device to make sure it is functioning properly, as required in Sec. 300.113(b).

(c) Individual related services terms defined. The terms used in this definition are defined as follows:

(1) Audiology includes—
(i) Identification of children with hearing loss;
(ii) Determination of the range, nature, and degree of hearing loss, including referral for medical or other professional attention for the habilitation of hearing;
(iii) Provision of habilitative activities, such as language habilitation, auditory training, speech reading (lip-reading), hearing evaluation, and speech conservation;
(iv) Creation and administration of programs for prevention of hearing loss;
(v) Counseling and guidance of children, parents, and teachers regarding hearing loss; and
(vi) Determination of children's needs for group and individual amplification, selecting and fitting an appropriate aid, and evaluating the effectiveness of amplification.

(2) Counseling services means services provided by qualified social workers, psychologists, guidance counselors, or other qualified personnel.

(3) Early identification and assessment of disabilities in children means the implementation of a formal plan for identifying a disability as early as possible in a child's life.

(4) Interpreting services includes—
(i) The following, when used with respect to children who are deaf or hard of hearing: Oral transliteration services, cued language transliteration services, sign language transliteration and interpreting services, and transcription services, such as communication access real-time translation (CART), C-Print, and TypeWell; and
(ii) Special interpreting services for children who are deaf-blind.

(5) Medical services means services provided by a licensed physician to determine a child's medically related disability that results in the child's need for special education and related services.

(6) Occupational therapy—

(i) Means services provided by a qualified occupational therapist; and

(ii) Includes—

(a) Improving, developing, or restoring functions impaired or lost through illness, injury, or deprivation;

(b) Improving ability to perform tasks for independent functioning if functions are impaired or lost; and

(c) Preventing, through early intervention, initial or further impairment or loss of function.

(7) Orientation and mobility services—

(i) Means services provided to blind or visually impaired children by qualified personnel to enable those students to attain systematic orientation to and safe movement within their environments in school, home, and community; and

(ii) Includes teaching children the following, as appropriate:

(a) Spatial and environmental concepts and use of information received by the senses (such as sound, temperature and vibrations) to establish, maintain, or regain orientation and line of travel (e.g., using sound at a traffic light to cross the street);

(b) To use the long cane or a service animal to supplement visual travel skills or as a tool for safely negotiating the environment for children with no available travel vision;

(c) To understand and use remaining vision and distance low vision aids; and

(d) Other concepts, techniques, and tools.

(8)

(i) Parent counseling and training means assisting parents in understanding the special needs of their child;

(ii) Providing parents with information about child development; and

(iii) Helping parents to acquire the necessary skills that will allow them to support the implementation of their child's IEP or IFSP.

(9) Physical therapy means services provided by a qualified physical therapist.

(10) Psychological services includes—

(i) Administering psychological and educational tests, and other assessment procedures;

(ii) Interpreting assessment results;

(iii) Obtaining, integrating, and interpreting information about child behavior and conditions relating to learning;

(iv) Consulting with other staff members in planning school programs to meet the special educational needs of children as indicated by psychological tests, interviews, direct observation, and behavioral evaluations;

(v) Planning and managing a program of psychological services, including psychological counseling for children and parents; and

(vi) Assisting in developing positive behavioral intervention strategies.

(11) Recreation includes—

(i) Assessment of leisure function;

(ii) Therapeutic recreation services;

(iii) Recreation programs in schools and community agencies; and

(iv) Leisure education.

(12) Rehabilitation counseling services means services provided by qualified personnel in individual or group sessions that focus specifically on career development, employment

preparation, achieving independence, and integration in the workplace and community of a student with a disability. The term also includes vocational rehabilitation services provided to a student with a disability by vocational rehabilitation programs funded under the Rehabilitation Act of 1973, as amended, 29 U.S.C. 701 et seq.

(13) School health services and school nurse services means health services that are designed to enable a child with a disability to receive FAPE as described in the child's IEP. School nurse services are services provided by a qualified school nurse. School health services are services that may be provided by either a qualified school nurse or other qualified person.

(14) Social work services in schools includes—
    (i) Preparing a social or developmental history on a child with a disability;
    (ii) Group and individual counseling with the child and family;
    (iii) Working in partnership with parents and others on those problems in a child's living situation (home, school, and community) that affect the child's adjustment in school;
    (iv) Mobilizing school and community resources to enable the child to learn as effectively as possible in his or her educational program; and
    (v) Assisting in developing positive behavioral intervention strategies.

(15) Speech-language pathology services includes—
    (i) Identification of children with speech or language impairments;
    (ii) Diagnosis and appraisal of specific speech or language impairments;
    (iii) Referral for medical or other professional attention necessary for the habilitation of speech or language impairments;
    (iv) Provision of speech and language services for the habilitation or prevention of communicative impairments; and
    (v) Counseling and guidance of parents, children, and teachers regarding speech and language impairments.

(16) Transportation includes—
    (i) Travel to and from school and between schools;
    (ii) Travel in and around school buildings; and
    (iii) Specialized equipment (such as special or adapted buses, lifts, and ramps), if required to provide special transportation for a child with a disability.
    (Authority: 20 U.S.C. 1401(26))

Acronyms Frequently Used in Special Education

A

AAD	adaptive assistive devices
AAT	advanced academic training
ABA	applied behavior analysis
ABD	antisocial behavior disorders
ABE	adult basic education
AC	alternative certification
ACROS	automated cross-referencing occupational system
ACT	American College Testing
AD	attachment disorder
ADA	Americans with Disabilities Act; average daily attendance
ADC	Aid to Dependent Children
ADD	attention deficit disorder
ADHD	attention deficit hyperactivity disorder

ADL	activities of daily living
ADM	average daily membership
ADR	alternative dispute resolution
ADVOC-NET	adult vocational network
AEA	acquired eleptiform aphasia (Landau-Kleffner syndrome)
AEP	alternative education placement
AFDC	Aid to Families with Dependent Children
AFS	adult and family services
AG	annual goal
AHSD	adult high school diploma
AI	auditorily impaired
AIDS	acquired immune deficiency syndrome
AIT	Agency for Instructional Technology
ALO	alternative learning options
ALS	advanced life support
AMD	alternative mobility device
AP	advanced placement
APD	antisocial personality disorder; auditory processing disorder
APE	adaptive physical education
APPE	average per pupil expenditure
ARD	admission, review, and dismissal [committee]
ARP	advisory review panel
ASC	advanced study center
ASD	autism spectrum disorder
ASDO	alternative service delivery options
ASL	American Sign Language
AT	assistive technology
ATC	area technical center; alternative teacher certification
ATCP	alternative teacher certification program
AU	autistic
AUT	autism
AVTI	area vocational technical institute
AYP	annual yearly progress
B	
BAC	behavior adjustment class
BASIS	Basic Adult Skills Inventory System
BD	behaviorally disordered; behavior disorders; brain damaged
BEP	behavioral education plan
BEST	basic education study team
BETAC	bilingual education technical assistance centers
BI	brain injury
BIA	Brain Injury Association; Bureau of Indian Affairs
BIL	bilingual
BIP	behavior intervention plan
BLS	basic life support
BMP	behavior management plan
BOCES	Board of Comprehensive Education Services (New York State)
C	
CA	chronological age
CAI	computer-assisted instruction
CAM	certificate of advanced mastery

CAP	central auditory processing
CAPD	central auditory processing disorders; see also APD (auditory processing disorder)
CAT	committee on accessible transportation
CBA	curriculum-based assessment
CBM	curriculum-based measurement
CC	cross categorical
CD	communication development; conduct disorder
CDA	child development associate
CDRC	child development and rehabilitation center
CDS	child development specialist
CFLA	community and family living amendments
CFR	Code of Federal Regulations
CHAP	child health assurance program
CHD	Center on Human Development
CHI	closed head injury
CIL	Center for Independent Living
CIM	certificate of initial mastery
CLAS	culturally and linguistically appropriate services
CLD	culturally and linguistically diverse
CMHP	community mental health program
CNS	central nervous system
COTA	certified occupational therapist assistant
CP	cerebral palsy
CPPC	cooperative personnel planning council
CPSE	committee on preschool special education
CSA	childhood sexual abuse
CSE	case study evaluation; committee on special education
CSEF	Center for Special Education Finance
CSPD	comprehensive system of personnel development
CSS	community support service
CTT	community transition team
D	
D	deaf
D&E	diagnosis and evaluation
DAP	developmentally appropriate practices
DARTS	day and residential treatment services
DAS	developmental apraxia of speech
DB; DBL	deaf-blind
DCD	developmental coordination disorder
DD	developmental disabilities; developmentally delayed
DDC	developmental disabilities council
DDD	division of developmental disabilities
DHHAP	deaf and hard of hearing access program
DHR	Department of Human Resources
DI	direct instruction
DNR	do not resuscitate
DoDDS	U.S. Dept. of Defense Dependent Schools
DOE	Department of Education
DON	determination of need
DREDF	Disability Rights Education and Defense Fund

DRG	diagnostically related groups
DS	direction service
DSM	Diagnostic and Statistical Manual [of Mental Disorders]
E	
EBD	emotional and behavioral disorders
EC	early childhood; exceptional child[ren]
ECE	early childhood education
ECI	early childhood intervention
ECSE	early childhood special education
ECT	early childhood team
ED	emotionally disturbed; emotional disorders; U.S. Department of Education
EDGAR	Education Department General Administrative Regulations
EEs	essential elements
EEN	exceptional education needs
EFA	experimental functional analysis
EI	early intervention
EI/ECSE	early intervention/early childhood special education
ELL	English language learner
EMH	educable mentally handicapped
EMR	educably mentally retarded
EMT	emergency medical treatment
EPSDT	early periodic screening diagnosis and treatment program
EQ	exceptional quality
ERC	education resource center
ERIC	Educational Resources Information Center
ESA	education service agency
ESC	education service center
ESD	education service district
ESE	exceptional student education
ESEA	Elementary and Secondary Education Act
ESL	English as a second language
ESOL	English for speakers of other languages
ESY	extended school year
ETP	effective teaching practices
EYS	extended year services (ECSE)
F	
FAIP	functional assessment and intervention program
FAPE	free appropriate public education
FAST	functional academic skills test
FBA	functional behavior assessment
FC	facilitated communication; foster care
FDAB	Fair Dismissal Appeals Board
FERPA	Family Educational Rights to Privacy Act (aka the Buckley Amendment)
FIPSA	Fund for the Improvement of Postsecondary Education
FLSA	Fair Labor Standards Act
FMLA	Family Medical Leave Act
FR	Federal Register
FSA	Family Support Act
FSHA	first-source hiring agreement
FSD	flexible service delivery model
FTE	full-time equivalent

FY	fiscal year
G	
GAPS	guardianship, advocacy, and protective services
GSE	generic special education
GT	gifted and talented
H	
HBCU	historically black colleges and universities
HI	health impaired; hearing impaired
HOH	hard of hearing
HOTS	higher-order thinking skills
HS	head start; high school
HSC	high school completion
I	
IAES	interim alternative educational setting
IASA	Improving America's Schools Act
ICC	interagency coordinating council
ICD	international code of diseases
ICDP	individual career development plans
ICF	intermediate care facility
ICFMR	intermediate care facility for mental retardation
IDEA	Individuals with Disabilities Education Act
IDELR	Individuals with Disabilities Education Law Report (from LRP Pubs.)
IED	intermittent explosive disorder
IEE	independent education evaluation
IEP	individualized education program
IEPC	individualized educational planning committee
IEU	intermediate educational unit
IFA	individualized functional assessment
IFSP	individualized family service plan
IHCP	individualized health care plan
IHE	institution of higher education
IHO	impartial hearing officer
IHP	individualized habilitation program or plan
IHTP	individualized habilitation and treatment plan
ILC	independent living center
ILP	independent living plan
ILT	instructional leadership training
IMC	instructional materials center
IML	instructional materials laboratory
IPE	individualized plan for employment
IPL	initial program load
IPP	individualized program plan
IQ	intelligence quotient
ISP	individualized service plan
ISS	in-school suspension
ITH	intensive training home
ITIP	instructional theory into practice
ITP	individualized transition plan (similar to IEP)
J	
JDRP	joint dissemination review panel
JOBS	job opportunities and basic skills

JJAEP	juvenile justice alternative education
JTPA	Job Training Partnership Act
L	
LA	language arts
LD	learning disabilities; learning disabled
LDA	Learning Disabilities Association
LDP	language development program
LEA	local education agency
LEDS	law enforcement data system
LEP	limited English proficient
LICC	local interagency coordinating council
LIFE	living in functional environments
LoF	Letter of Finding issued by the Office for Civil Rights (OCR)
LPTA	licensed physical therapy assistant
LRE	least restrictive environment
LSSP	licensed specialist in school psychology
LTCF	long-term care facility
LTCT	long-term care and treatment
M	
MA	mental age
MBD	minimal brain dysfunction
MBO	management by objective
MDC	multidisciplinary conference
MDT	multidisciplinary team; manifest determination team
M/ED	mental or emotional disturbance
MESC	migrant education service center
MFCU	medically fragile children's unit
MH	multiply handicapped
MHM	multihandicapped mainstream
MHMR	mental health mental retardation
MI	multiple intelligences
MIS	management information systems
MMR	mild mental retardation
MMS	mastery management system
MR	mentally retarded or mental retardation
MR/DD	mentally retarded/developmentally disabled
MR/MED	mentally retarded and mentally or emotionally disturbed (sometimes referred to as dual diagnosis)
MSDD	multisystem developmental disorder
MSRTS	migrant student record transfer system
MST	multisystemic therapy
N	
NCES	National Center for Education Statistics
NCLB; NCLBA	No Child Left Behind Act
NDT	neurodevelopmental treatment
NEA	National Education Association
NICU	neonatal intensive care unit
NSBA	National School Boards Association
O	
O&M	orientation and mobility
OCD	obsessive compulsive disorder

OCR	Office of Civil Rights
ODAS	occupational data analysis system
ODD	oppositional defiant disorder
OE	open entries
OECD	Organization for Economic Cooperation and Development
OH	orthopedically handicapped
OHI	other health impairments
OMI	other minorities
OSEP	Office of Special Education Programs, U.S. Department of Education
OT	occupational therapy/therapist
OT/PT	occupational therapy/physical therapy

P

P and A	protection and advocacy
PACER	Parent Advocacy Coalition for Educational Rights Center
PALS	peer-assisted learning system
PAVE	parents advocating for vocational education
PCA	personal care attendant
PCD	perceptual communicative disability
PDAS	professional development and appraisal system
PDD	pervasive development disorder
PDD-NOS	pervasive development disorder—not otherwise specified
PEATC	Parent Education Advocacy Training Center
PECS	picture exchange communication system
PEIMS	public education information management system
PEL	present education level
PERS	public employees retirement system
PET	pupil evaluation team
PIC	private industry council
PIQ	performance IQ
PLATO	programmed logic automatic teaching operations
PLI	pragmatic language impairment
PLOP	present level of performance
PPCD	preschool program for children with disabilities
PPS	pupil personnel services
PRE-K	pre-kindergarten
PT	physical therapy/therapist
PTA	physical therapist assistant; post-traumatic amnesia
PTG	parent teacher group
PTSD	post-traumatic stress disorder
PTT	planning and placement team
PVS	persistent vegetative state; private vocational schools
PY	project year

Q

QAFB	questions about functional behavior
QMRP	qualified mental retardation professional

R

RAD	reactive attachment disorder
RCF	residential care facility
RCH	residential care home
R&D	research and development
RDD	reading disorder-dyslexia

REBT	rational emotive behavior therapy
REI	regular education initiative
RFP	request for proposal
RMT	regional management team
RRC	regional resource centers
RSP	resource specialist (regional term)
R&T	research and training
RTC	residential treatment center
RTH	residential training home
RTI	response to intervention
RWQC	regional workforce quality committee
S	
SAT	scholastic aptitude test
SB L-M	Stanford-Binet, form L-M (language/memory)
SBE; SBOE	state board of education
SBS	schoolwide behavior supports
SDA	service delivery area
SDC	special day class
SDE	self-directed employment
SE	special education
SEA	state education agency; state education association
SECC	special education child count
SECTION 504	a part of the Rehabilitation Act of 1973 making it illegal for any organization receiving federal funds to discriminate against a person solely on the basis of disability
SED	seriously emotionally disturbed
SEMS	special education management system
SENCO	special education needs coordinator
SENG	supporting the emotional needs of the gifted
SERVE	secondary education reporting of vocational enrollment
SI	speech impaired
SIB	self-injurious behavior
SICC	state interagency coordinating council
SIG	state improvement grant
SILP	semi-independent living program
SIP	state improvement plan
SIS	shared information systems
SLC	structured learning center
SLD	specific learning disability
SLP	speech-language pathologist
SLPA	speech-language pathologist assistant
SLR	state liaison representative
SPeNSE	study of personnel needs in special education
SOL	standards of learning
SOSCF	state offices for services to children and families
SPD	semantic pragmatic disorder
SPED	special education
SPLD	semantic pragmatic language disorder
SSA	Social Security Act; Social Security Administration
SSBD	septimatic screening for behavior disorders
SSD	Social Security disability
SSDI	Social Security disability income

SSI	statewide systemic initiative; Supplemental Security Income
SST	student study team; student support team
STO	short-term objective
T	
TAG	talented and gifted
TBI	traumatic brain injury
TDD	telecommunication devices for the deaf
TESOL	teachers of English for speakers of other languages
TIP	teacher improvement process
TLC	therapeutic learning center
TMH	trainable mentally handicapped
TMR	trainably mentally retarded
TOVA	test of variable attention
TPP	transition planning process
TTY	teletypewriter (phone system for deaf individuals—see TDD)
U	
UAF	university affiliated facility
UCE	university centers for excellence
V	
VAC	vocational adjustment counselor; vocational adjustment class
VCD	volitional conduct disorder
VEDS	vocational education data systems
VI	visually impaired
VRD	vocational rehabilitation division
VSA	very special arts
W	
WAC	work activity center
WISC-R	Weschler Intelligence Scale for Children—Revised
WISC-III	Weschler Intelligence Scale for Children—Third Edition
WOD	written output disorder
WQC	workplace quality council
WRAP	wraparound program
Y	
YTP	youth transition program

Retrieved 4/1/06 from http://www.cec.sped.org/Content/NavigationMenu/NewsIssues/TeachingLearningCenter/ Special_Education_Acronyms_and_Abbreviations.htm.

2

The Individualized Education Program (IEP)

"Let us think of education as the means of developing our greatest abilities, because in each of us there is a private hope and dream which, fulfilled, can be translated into benefit for everyone and greater strength for our nation."

John F. Kennedy (1917–1963)

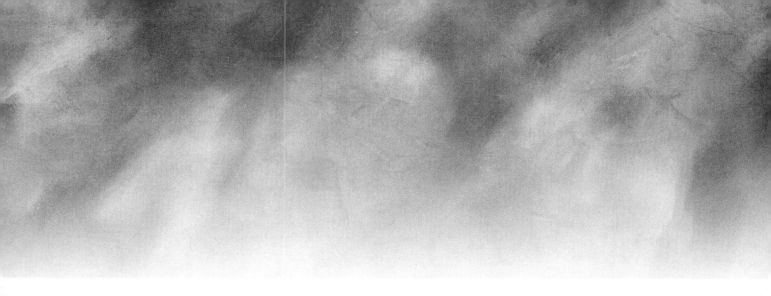

CHAPTER OBJECTIVES

- Review special education legislation of 2004
- Review IEP legal issues
- Review IEP pragmatic issues

Before reading this chapter, take a moment to note what comes to mind when you think of individualized education programs (IEPs) for students with disabilities. Do you know the legal mandates and timelines according to the public law, IDEA 2004? What type of experience have you had with the IEP process? Have you been a participant or an observer in this process? Record your reflections and revisit your response as you read this chapter.

INTRODUCTION

The intent of this chapter is to provide you with an overview of the individualized education program (IEP) process. The IEP is both a document and a process (National Association of State Directors of Special Education, 1996). The IEP was first conceived under PL 94–142 to address the need to individualize instruction for students with special needs. There have been several amendments to this law, with the most recent revision found in the IDEA 2004 (PL 108–446).

A student who has an IEP document is identified as a student in need of special education services, and one whose individualized education program has specific legal mandates that must be addressed. To help you to understand the IEP process this chapter will first provide background information on special education legislation in 2004 (see Figure 2.1).

Second, it will discuss legal issues about the IEP in regard to referrals, parental consent, evaluation, team coordination, procedural safeguards, eligibility determination, measurable goals, related services, placement recommendations, process to report student's progress, implementation, and reevaluation.

Third, to help you implement the process, this chapter presents practical tips for improving teacher/parent interactions, preparing for IEP meetings, enhancing the special education teacher's role at IEP meetings, and creating effective IEP team meetings.

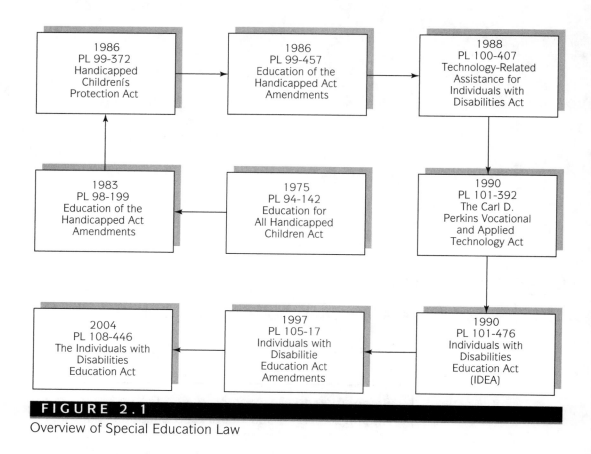

FIGURE 2.1

Overview of Special Education Law

SPECIAL EDUCATION LEGISLATION IN 2004

Congress reauthorized IDEA as the Individuals with Disabilities Education Act of 2004 (PL 108–446). Some provisions went into effect immediately, while changes in the IEP were not required until July 2005. The final regulations were issued in August 2006. (The full text of the law is available at http://www.copyright.gov/legislation/p1108-446. html#306). Several key provisions in the law are presented here and are summarized in Figure 2.2.

The Individual with Disabilities Education Act (IDEA) of 2004 requires that for each student needing special education, an individualized education program (IEP) be developed. It must include a statement of the individual's present level of academic achievement and functional performance, as well as measurable annual goals. Benchmarks or short-term objectives are no longer required. Only students who are identified as needing to take alternate assessments because they are working toward alternate standards need short-term objectives included in the IEP along with measurable annual goals.

The IEP team, whose members consist of parents or guardians and representatives from the local education agency, determine the annual goals based on assessment data. The student's developmental, academic, and functional needs and strengths are considered by the IEP team, as well as the placement where the student's needs are to be addressed: the general education and/or the special education environments. After reviewing the data, the student's IEP team also determines the program, or type of service delivery model, that is needed for the student to successfully achieve the annual

Issue	Change
IEP team	Teams do not have to include a general education teacher if the student is not participating in the general education curriculum or if there is written consent from the parent that the general education teachers do not have to attend the meeting. If appropriate, the general education teacher may submit information to be considered for the development of the IEP. The team may convene through video or phone format.
Assistive technology device	No change in defining assitive technology devices. The law stipulates that schools are not financially responsible for medical devices such as cochlear implants.
Highly qualified teachers	This term was not previously used in the law. Language now mirrors "No Child Left Behind." For new special education teachers, the law requires a bachelor's degree, certification in special education, and competence documentation in subject matter.
Parent	Defines parent to include a natural, foster, or adoptive parent, a guardian, or a relative.
Learning disability	Definition is unchanged, but a discrepancy model is not required in determining the presence of a learning disability. The IEP team can determine eligibility based on the student's success with research-based intervention efforts.
Paperwork reduction	Option of 3-year IEPs (with parent consent) to be tested in 15 states.
Disciplinary actions	Student may be moved to an alternative setting whether or not the behavior is a manifestation of the student's disability, if special circumstances apply (e.g., drugs, weapons, bodily harm). Special education services must continue, although placement may change.

FIGURE 2.2

IDEA 2004

FIGURE 2.3

Did You Know?

Over 6 million students in the United States have an IEP.
Over 13% of students in elementary and secondary schools have an IEP.
Over 95% of students with an IEP are served in their general education community school.

goals. All of these determinations are included on a written document called the individualized education program (IEP; see Figure 2.3).

For children between the ages of 3 and 5, the individualized family service plan (IFSP) may substitute for the IEP if all people involved in the decision-making process agree to this.

In providing a free and appropriate public education (FAPE) in the least restrictive environment (LRE) for a student with an exceptionality, the team may agree at the annual IEP meeting, with parent permission, to amend an IEP without convening the whole IEP team, if change is necessary in its implementation. The IEP team members may revisit their decision regarding placement and objectives whenever they consider it appropriate. The law also allows, if the parent agrees, alternative methods of conducting IEP meetings, such as via phone or videoconference. An alternative IEP meeting may be appropriate when there are no changes in the type of service a student is receiving and the placement of the student.

HIGHLY QUALIFIED TEACHER

IDEA 2004 includes the criteria for being considered a highly qualified teacher in special education. This qualification is based on many factors. In general, all teachers must have a bachelor's degree, state certification or have passed a state licensing exam, and have a license to teach in the state. There are additional requirements based on whether one is teaching multiple subjects, teaching to alternate standards, and whether one is new or not new to the profession. We advise you to check with your local authority regarding teacher certification and state employment requirements.

INDIVIDUALIZED EDUCATION PROGRAM

This chapter provides more detailed information on the IEP, and some key changes in IEP planning are mentioned here. One provision is that the IEP must include measurable annual goals; short-term objectives or benchmarks are not required except in specific cases. Special education programs are required to provide parents (defined as the natural, foster, and adoptive) or guardians with regular reports on the progress of each special education student. However, when there is a need to change an IEP, the IEP team can now accomplish this with permission from the parent and the school without a formal IEP meeting. When the IEP team convenes for the annual meeting, not all teachers have to be present if their content is not being discussed. If not attending the IEP meeting, general education teachers may choose to submit in writing any comments or discussion items. The IEP team needs to address the functional, academic, and developmental needs of the student in developing the IEP.

Language in IDEA authorizes 15 states to pilot a multiyear IEP (not greater than 3 years) that allows for longer-term educational planning. This effort endeavors to reduce paperwork and the amount of noninstructional time teachers spend on this effort.

RESPONSE TO INTERVENTION (RTI) AND LEARNING DISABILITY

With respect to the definition of a learning disability, it remains unchanged with IDEA 2004, but the IEP team can evaluate a student by determining the individual's success with research-based, scientific interventions without having to consider a discrepancy between achievement and ability levels for a determination of a learning disability. This change allows the IEP team more flexibility in determining the appropriate educational program for a student with a disability. When using the response to intervention (RTI) model for determining a learning disability, the general education teacher needs to present to the team evidence of the interventions attempted and the lack of success on the student's part for the team to determine a learning disability. States are encouraged to develop statewide criteria that would provide consistency within each state in determining the presence of a learning disability. Figure 2.4 summarizes the RTI approach.

Three-Tier Approach to RTI Includes: Early Universal Screening, Progress Monitoring, Problem Solving at Each Level, Collaboration, and Research-Based Interventions	
Tier I	CORE INSTRUCTION FOR ALL STUDENTS High-quality instruction in general education Preventive, Proactive RTI focus: All students achieve benchmarks Early universal screening Differentiated instruction Effective, research-based instructional/behavioral interventions
Tier II	SUPPLEMENTAL INSTRUCTION FOR SOME STUDENTS (AT–RISK) Focused instruction in general education for students who demonstrate difficulty Targeted group interventions RTI focus: Strategic supplemental instruction Core and supplemental instructional materials Frequent progress monitoring On-going assessment of student performance
Tier III	INTENSIVE INSTRUCTION FOR INDIVIDUAL STUDENTS Continuous assessment by team as a result of inadequate response to research-based interventions, lack of progress Individual focused intensive intervention applied with fidelity (Not special education) RTI focus: Use of data to make instructional decisions Consideration of referral for special education when there is a marked lack of response to interventions, and the student's achievement remains significantly below benchmarks

FIGURE 2.4

Response to Intervention (RTI)

Source: Allan Lloyd-Jones, Special Education Consultant, California Department of Education.

ENGLISH LANGUAGE LEARNERS

Because the fastest growing populations in many parts of our country are English language learners, IDEA 2004 suggests that greater efforts are needed to prevent the mislabeling of limited-English-speaking students as special education students, along with inappropriate placement in special education classes. We suggest the team consult with a teacher specializing in working with second-language learners in understanding a specific student's learning issues before considering the student for special education placement. The law also states that because English language students in special education have a higher dropout rate than English language students in general education, schools should increase recruitment efforts for culturally diverse teachers as role models to improve graduation rates and provide transition services for these students.

DISCIPLINE PROVISIONS

IDEA 2004 includes several changes to the discipline provisions previously addressed in IDEA 1997. Local school authorities can decide on a case-by-case basis whether or not a change in placement is warranted for a special education student in violation of a school code of conduct. The local education agency reviews all information in a manifestation hearing, including whether or not the cause of the student's conduct is a result of the disability or the result of an IEP not implemented. If the special education agency decides that the violation of a student code of conduct is a manifestation of the student's disability, the IEP team conducts a functional behavioral assessment and implements a behavioral intervention plan. A special education student may be moved to an interim placement for 45 school days when the student inflicts bodily harm on another at school, brings drugs on school premises, or possesses a weapon on school property. We suggest the team consult the law before making a decision about an interim placement.

ASSISTIVE TECHNOLOGY

IDEA 2004 maintains previous language regarding assistive technology, but the law now stipulates that schools are not financially responsible for medical devices surgically implanted, such as cochlear implants. As the technology develops, the law may need to address additional issues regarding financial responsibilities.

In considering assistive technology, the teacher's focus is on technology that augments a student's performance, bypasses a disability, or compensates for a disability. Assistive technology (AT) is considered for a student when an assessment team provides data demonstrating the need for AT for a student to achieve IEP goals. We recommend the assessment team include an individual who is certified in assistive technology to provide the expertise needed in the decision-making process. The IEP team's decision about the use of assistive technology must be reflected on the IEP. Assistive technology addresses assessment, services (purchasing, adapting, maintenance, training), and technology devices (not medical) that provide instructional support for students. Because there is no one technology solution for all students, the teacher needs to consider designing lessons that allow for multiple means of representation (acquiring the information), expression (ways to demonstrate learning), and engagement (ways to motivate) to allow for all students' individual differences to be addressed (Center for Applied Special Technology, 2007). This orientation to technology is called *universal design*. Assistive technology is discussed in depth in Chapter 6. Figure 2.5 asks you to reflect on IDEA 2004 and your knowledge of special education.

IEP LEGAL ISSUES

According to IDEA 2004, either parents or the state education agency (SEA), other state agency, or the local education agency (LEA) can do a referral, or a request for an initial evaluation to determine educational needs and eligibility for special education services. This means that a parent or school personnel such as teacher or school counselor could request an initial evaluation. The law establishes a time frame within which the evaluation must be completed. This time frame is 60 days after receiving parental consent, or if a particular state has an established time frame, that time frame may be used. Two specific situations where the time frame does not apply are addressed in the new law. The

FIGURE 2.5

Take a Moment

Think About	Reflect	Respond
Special education	Can you discuss the major components of IDEA 2004?	
	What areas of special education do you need more information about?	

first situation is when the student changes schools in the middle of an initial evaluation, and the second is when the parent repeatedly fails or refuses to produce the student for evaluation.

PARENTAL CONSENT

The law prohibits school districts from convening an IEP meeting, developing an IEP, and providing services without parental consent. However, the agency is not required to obtain parents' informed consent for initial evaluation if, despite reasonable efforts, the agency cannot locate the parent, the parent's rights have been ended, or the right to make educational decisions has been assigned by a court to another individual. Typically, reevaluation shall occur once a year and definitely should occur at least once every 3 years, unless parent and LEA agree that the reevaluation is not necessary.

EVALUATION

After a student has been referred to special education, you need to communicate with the parents to discuss the assessment process, which requires written parental permission before any evaluation for special education eligibility can take place. Specific tests and the process for collecting all data need to be discussed. Appropriate assessment information includes both testing and observation of a student's educational and behavioral performance by more than one person. In some cases, a functional assessment of behavior needs to be conducted.

IDEA 2004 states that a variety of assessments must be provided in "the language and form most likely to yield accurate information on what the child knows and can do academically, developmentally, and functionally, unless it is not feasible to so provide or administer." It is your responsibility as the special education teacher to assess the academic achievement levels of the student who is being referred for special education and related services. The special education teacher may also conduct behavioral observations and a functional assessment of behavior. The IDEA 2004 "exclusionary language" states that a child cannot be considered to have a disability if the determining factor is "lack of appropriate instruction in reading." In making the determination if a child has a specific learning disability, the law states that a local education agency (LEA) may use "a process that determines if the child responds to scientific, research-based intervention" as a part of the special education evaluation. This could mean that assessments to determine whether a child has a specific learning disability may vary a great deal from one school district to another. As mentioned previously, states are encouraged to develop statewide criteria that would provide consistency within the state in determining the presence of a learning disability.

After the assessments are completed, the IEP team meets to determine special education eligibility, develop the student's individualized education program (IEP), and determine placement recommendation.

TEAM COORDINATION

Typically, the IEP team consists of the parent, administrator or someone designated by the administrator to represent the LEA, school psychologist (note—this person may also be the designated LEA representative), special education teacher, and sometimes the student. Representatives from "designated instructional services" (DIS) or related services (defined in the IDEA regulations as services that supplement the educational services provided in the classroom) may also be present at the IEP meeting. For example, participating IEP members may include someone from counseling services, medical services, occupational therapy, parent counseling and training, physical therapy, psychological services, recreation, rehabilitative counseling services, school health services, social work services in schools, and/or speech pathology.

IEP team attendance, under IDEA 2004, explains who does not have to be at the meeting and under what circumstances. The law clearly indicates that the parents and a representative from the LEA need to attend the IEP team meeting. Parents must agree and consent in writing for a team member not to attend or to be excused from attendance if the member submits written input to the parents and team before the meeting.

PROCEDURAL SAFEGUARDS

Typically in an IEP meeting, parents' procedural safeguards are discussed first. Under IDEA 2004, procedural safeguards must be provided to each parent of a student with a disability once per year. Sometimes you may want to sit next to the parents when reviewing the procedural safeguards, or you may want the parent to sit next to the person chairing the meeting. People tend to look at the person chairing the meeting, and the parent will also benefit from that eye contact (Johns, Crowley, & Guetzloe, 2002).

DETERMINATION OF ELIGIBILITY

The next segment of the IEP meeting focuses on the determination of eligibility for special education and related services, underscoring the child's learning needs. During this part of the IEP meeting, the conversation among all team members includes the sharing of the evaluation results of present levels of educational performance, including how the disability affects involvement and progress in the general education curriculum (see Figure 2.6).

Therefore, determination of eligibility for special education is three pronged: (1) student meets criteria for one or more disabilities as defined by law, (2) the data show how the student's disability adversely affects educational performance, and (3) the student is in need of special education, or specially designed instruction. Thus, special education is not defined by who is providing it, or where it is provided. Specially designed instruction is related to delivery of instruction.

If eligibility for special education and related services is determined, based on the assessment results, then the next step is to discuss the measurable IEP goals and objectives. According to Johns et al. (2002, p. 56), "Students must gain meaningful benefit from an IEP. Clearly written goals and objectives can provide us with the information needed to show that benefit."

FIGURE 2.6

Key Facts on Present Levels of Educational Performance (PLEP)

1. Present level of educational performance (PLEP) provides baseline data on a student's educational performance.
2. PLEP data helps you plan appropriate instruction for your students.
3. PLEP data should include a description of how your student's disability affects his or her educational performance.
4. To determine PLEP, use:
   - Formal assessments: standardized test results from state and district examinations.
   - Informal assessments: student work samples, teacher observations, portfolios, teacher-made tests.
   - Data and assessments from nonacademic as well as academic areas such as daily living skills, communication ability, emotional and behavioral functioning, and social skills.

MEASURABLE GOALS

At the IEP meeting, the special education teacher is responsible for providing suggestions for the annual IEP goals. We strongly recommend that you prepare and write down suggested measurable goals for the student based on the assessment data collected before the meeting. Best practice would be to discuss these ideas with parents before the meeting. You can bring a written draft of goals to the meeting and write "draft" across the page. During the meeting, any modifications to your draft goals must be included. When the IEP team has agreed on the goals for the student, enter the goals on the IEP form. In some cases, you can cross out the word "draft" on the top of your page and initial it.

WRITING IEP GOALS

Writing annual measurable IEP goals is the responsibility of the special educator. Be sure to write goals in terms that are observable and quantifiable. Research tells us that four components are needed in measurable goals. These components are: (1) the student's name, (2) the target behavior or what the student is expected to accomplish, (3) the conditions under which the behavior will be performed, and (4) the criteria for acceptable performance or how well the task is to be performed. Figure 2.7 presents guidelines for writing IEP goals. IDEA 2004 now requires that academic and functional goals be written as part of the IEP. Figure 2.8 provides a practical procedure for monitoring IEP goals.

Some school districts are using electronic IEPS, in which goals are typed into a computer right onto the IEP form during the meeting. In any case, the critical point to remember is that the student's goals are determined and written during the IEP meeting and input from all team members must be considered and discussed.

Sample Annual Goal:

Dori (**WHO**) will add two-digit numbers (**DOES WHAT**) by June 1, 2009 (**WHEN**), when given 10 two-digit addition computation problems (**GIVEN WHAT**), with at least 80% accuracy in 3 out of 5 trials (**HOW MUCH**) as measured by a teacher-made written test (**HOW WILL IT BE MEASURED**).

* WHO:	Student	Student's name
* DOES WHAT:	Observable behavior	Describes what the student will do to complete goal
* WHEN:	By reporting date	Timeline
* GIVEN WHAT:	Conditions	Describes what needs to be in place for the goal to be completed
* HOW MUCH:	Mastery	Describes the level of performance needed for the goal to be considered mastered or achieved
	Criteria	Describes how many times the behavior must be observed for the goal to be considered completed
* HOW WILL IT BE MEASURED:	Performance data	Describes how the performance data will be collected

FIGURE 2.7

Guidelines for Writing IEP Goals

Source: Adapted from *Handbook of Goals and Objectives Related to Essential State of California Content Standards* (2004), compiled by the Association of California School Administrators (ACSA) and the California Association of Resource Specialists and Special Education Teachers (CARS+), pp. 12–13.

MONITORING IEP GOALS

Name _____   Special Ed. Teacher _____

DOB _____   Grade _____ Placement _____

Phone _____   IEP Due Date _____ 3 Yr. _____

In each box below indicate the performance level each month as a percentage and indicate by a plus sign (+) if progress is demonstrated or a minus sign (−) if progress is not demonstrated.

Goal # 1:

Sept.	Oct.	Nov.	Dec.	Jan.	Feb.	Mar.	Apr.	May	June

Goal # 2:

Sept.	Oct.	Nov.	Dec.	Jan.	Feb.	Mar.	Apr.	May	June

Goal # 3:

Sept.	Oct.	Nov.	Dec.	Jan.	Feb.	Mar.	Apr.	May	June

Goal # 4:

Sept.	Oct.	Nov.	Dec.	Jan.	Feb.	Mar.	Apr.	May	June

Goal # 5:

Sept.	Oct.	Nov.	Dec.	Jan.	Feb.	Mar.	Apr.	May	June

Goal # 6:

Sept.	Oct.	Nov.	Dec.	Jan.	Feb.	Mar.	Apr.	May	June

FIGURE 2.8

Form for Monitoring IEP Goals

Source: Form designed and developed by Debra Baehler, M.A., Autism Specialist for Lassen County Office of Education, Susanville, CA.

RELATED SERVICES, ACCOMMODATIONS, AND MODIFICATIONS

After the IEP team members agree upon the goals, the next item usually discussed is related services and supplementary aids and services needed to advance toward annual goals, and to be involved and make progress in the general curriculum. This conversation would include "reasonable" and appropriate accommodations or adaptations to the classroom setting that will assist the student in learning skills, as well as modifications. Modifications are changes in the curriculum or the manner in which a student participates in district and/or state assessments.

Examples of accommodations include: preferential seating, use of a tape-recorder, additional time to complete tasks/take tests, a note-taker, a study guide, a graphic organizer or diagram of key content in a paragraph or book chapter, and textbooks on tape.

Examples of curriculum modifications for the student include: adapting materials to the appropriate instructional/independent reading level, providing writing frames, and changing the number and type of math problems required. The frequency and location of services and modifications are also determined by the IEP team and written on the IEP document.

Sometimes accommodations or modifications may have a financial impact for the school district, and a special education teacher may not be aware of this immediately. After reviewing the assessment data, if you have "reasonable" ideas for accommodations or modifications, we strongly suggest that you discuss them with your site administrator, particularly if there is a cost factor involved with implementing them, such as is the case with assistive technology devices. It is a good idea to try to brain storm various options on how to meet your student's needs before the IEP meeting, if at all possible.

OTHER SERVICE NEEDS

Communication, behavior, and occupational/physical needs are typical services and supports discussed at this point in the IEP. If the assessment data indicates communication issues, the speech/language therapist might provide IEP goals to be addressed in individual or group language sessions.

For culturally and linguistically diverse (CLD) exceptional students, we strongly recommend that the IEP include English language learning (ELL) assessment results and address learning needs by including annual measurable goals for language acquisition and development. This will further promote the collaboration between you, the special educator, and the bilingual/English as a second language (ESL) or English language learner (ELL) specialist.

A vision teacher might provide IEP goals for an individual working with Braille (instruction and assessment). After conducting an AT (assistive technology) assessment, the team might suggest a level of technology (high/low) needed for the student to meet annual goals.

When a behavioral assessment has been completed, the team might include behavior IEP goals, behavior strategies, and supports. A behavioral intervention plan needs to be based on a functional assessment of the student's behavior, assist the student in reaching behavior IEP goals, and drive a part of the student's curriculum (Johns, et al., 2002).

TRANSITION SERVICE NEEDS

If your student will turn 16 years old while this IEP is in effect, you will need to conduct age-appropriate transition assessments and prepare "draft" appropriate measurable postsecondary goals related to training, education, employment, and, where appropriate, independent skills. The IEP team will discuss transition service needs and, in addition to measurable postsecondary goals, identify in a transition statement the services and courses required to assist in reaching these goals. Transition service needs are updated annually.

EDUCATIONAL PLACEMENT RECOMMENDATION

After the IEP team members agree upon the measurable goals and related services needed, the next step is to determine the appropriate placement—that is, the least restrictive environment—where "specially designed instruction" can be provided. An important notion to consider when discussing placement is that the placement should be based on educational reasons. Is this the best place where goals and objectives can be met?

SERVICE DELIVERY MODELS

Once it has been determined that a student is in need of special education services, the IEP team selects the least restrictive environment (LRE) where the student's needs may be met and the IEP goals achieved. The general education classroom needs to be considered as the appropriate setting to meet the IEP goals prior to consideration of other placements. Placements for receiving special education services from least restrictive to most restrictive are: the general education classroom without modifications, general education classroom with supplementary aids and services, resource services, self-contained or special class, specialized setting outside the home school setting or general education building, and residential placement. The more common delivery models include the special education teacher providing consultation to the general classroom teacher, team-teaching or co-teaching situations, resource rooms, and self-contained classes (see Figure 2.9). The following sections provide an overview of each of these models.

CONSULTATION MODEL

With this model, the special education teacher works with the general education teacher in designing a class environment that promotes a student's success. The special education teacher shares information about the student's strengths and weaknesses, discusses ideas for assignments and assessments that promote learning, and offers information on

FIGURE 2.9

Service Delivery
Models

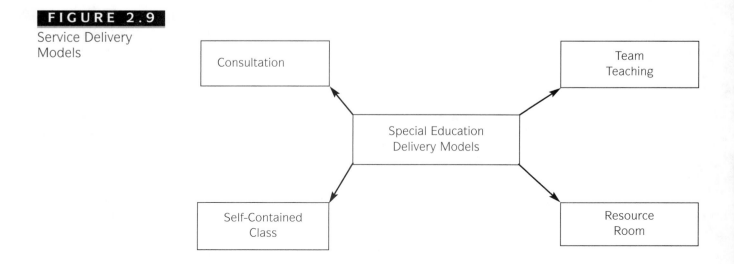

teaching strategies. The general education teacher is responsible for planning lessons based on the knowledge of the exceptionality, incorporating the most effective instructional strategy, and determining appropriate activities for the student to demonstrate competencies. Both teachers are responsible for monitoring the student's progress in this environment. Effective practice indicates that the stronger the collaborative relationship between the special education teacher and the general education teacher, the greater the possibility that the student will experience success in the general education classroom.

TEAM-TEACHING OR CO-TEACHING MODEL

A team-teaching environment involves the special educator teaching with the general education teacher in the core content classes. This collaborative model integrates the special education students with general education students for specific content. Both groups benefit from the support of a special educator and the general education teacher. An effective collaboration involves both teachers recognizing the strengths each is bringing to the team-teaching situation, and deciding how to use those strengths to support student achievement.

RESOURCE ROOM MODEL

Other students receive special education services through a resource room for a few hours a day. With this model, special education teachers offer small classes in the core content areas of English/reading, math, social studies, and science. Each school system makes decisions on what content the resource room environment offers and how much time a student spends in the resource room. Based on this, the IEP team reviews a student's assessment results to determine the specific content and the amount of time the student needs with a special education teacher in a resource room to achieve IEP goals.

SELF-CONTAINED CLASS

Some students may spend most of their day in self-contained classes because of the severity of their needs, which are documented through assessments and included on the IEP. The team selects this model when the support students need to achieve their goals is more than is available in a resource room or general education class environment. The IEP team can review the decision regarding placement in a self-contained class when evaluating a student's progress toward IEP goal achievement.

For some students, because of the severity of their needs that cannot be met in the local school, a more restrictive learning environment for a specific period of time, such as a residential school or a special school, may be needed.

The IEP team has the responsibility of monitoring the progress of each of the students and making determinations regarding changes in placements, when needed, to achieve IEP goals.

FIGURE 2.10
Take a Moment

Think About	Reflect	Respond
Delivery models	What models have you used or observed?	
	What models seem to be more successful with students as compared to others?	

Individualized Education Program Progress Report – Mastery of Objectives

Student: _____   DOB: _____   School: _____
Teacher: _____   Year: _____
Grade: _____

GOALS

Trimester	Performance				Goal Status				Measurement			
	Exceeded Objective	Objective Met	Making Progress	No Progress Observed	Continue Objective	Write New Objective	Objective Dropped		Standardized Test	Teacher-Made Test	Observation	Work Sample Portfolio

Synopsis of Objectives (rows numbered 1, 2, 3 for each goal group)

1
2
3
1
2
3
1
2
3
1
2
3
1
2
3
1
2
3

Skill Key for Behavior/Mainstream

3	= Consistently
2	= Frequently
1	= Occasionally
0	= Rarely

Student Behaviors

	Report Period		
	1	2	3

SOCIAL SKILLS

Gets along well with others
Displays positive classroom behavior
Displays positive playground behavior
Displays a positive attitude
Exhibits positive self concept
Shows self control
Accepts responsibility
Respects rights and property of others
Seeks help appropriately when needed

STUDY SKILLS

Completes and returns homework
Completes class work on time
Applies reading skills to content areas
Works independently
Works cooperatively in a group
Follows directions
Works neatly
Demonstrates proper use of materials
Contributes to class discussion
Organizes materials and work space
Uses time appropriately
Applies reasoning skills
Listens attentively

FIGURE 2.11

Sample Report Card

Source: Sample report card designed and developed by Laura Holman, M.A. (2005), Education Specialist Teacher for Chico Unified School District, Chico, CA.

PROCESS TO REPORT STUDENT'S PROGRESS TO PARENT

After the placement is determined, how the student's progress will be measured and reported to the parents is also decided upon by the IEP team and noted in a statement on the IEP document. It is mandatory that student progress reporting be addressed by the team. Figure 2.11 is an example of a form used for reporting to parents the progress of students with exceptional needs. Grading software is an efficient and time-saving method to monitor and report progress to parents, as well. Websites for grading software are included in Chapter 6, Figure 6.5, "Instructional Planning."

IMPLEMENTATION AND REEVALUATION OF THE IEP

Implementation of the individualized education program refers to placement after the IEP meeting. The parent's signature on the IEP document indicates written approval of the IEP and placement decision. Reevaluation occurs annually unless the parent and the local education agency (typically the school district) agree otherwise. Reevaluation should occur at least once every 3 years, unless the parent and school district agree that it is not necessary. Figure 2.12 asks you to reflect on the legal issues regarding the IEP process.

FIGURE 2.12

Take a Moment

Think About	Reflect	Respond
Individualized education program (IEP) process	What does the current law say about the IEP process?	
	What more do you want to know about the IEP process?	
	After a request for an initial evaluation is made, what do you do next?	
Individualized education program (IEP) team meetings	Have you ever observed or participated in an IEP meeting?	
	What role did you or the teacher play in this meeting?	
	What could you do to create an effective IEP team meeting?	
Individualized education program (IEP) document	Have you seen a completed IEP form or have you completedan IEP form?	
	What questions do you have about preparing and completing an IEP document?	

IEP Pragmatic Issues

Teacher/Parent Interactions

The reauthorization of IDEA 2004 emphasizes and empowers the parental role. Informed consent means that parents understand the information in the IEP documents that they are signing. As the special education teacher, we suggest that you take the time to talk to parents and develop a process to gather the best information for your students. The relationship that you build with your students' parents can directly affect your students' educational outcomes and attitudes, as well as their families' involvement with you personally as their teacher, and with the school program in general. We offer the following tips for improving teacher/parent relationships (see Figure 2.13).

It makes good sense to ask parents questions about their child, and not to assume you know what is really important to them regarding their child's education. You may be surprised at the number of different responses that parents will share with you. Oftentimes a parent's vision of success is an easy goal for a child to achieve. As a special education teacher, if you know what is important to parents, their personal markers of success, you can help your students to achieve these goals. If you never ask parents these simple questions, you are missing a wonderful opportunity to assist the performance of your students in their parents' eyes.

To help you begin a conversation with a parent before an IEP meeting takes place, see the list of parent interview questions (Figure 2.14). Responses to these questions provide information that is very useful and applicable to the IEP process, and these questions also promote better teacher and parent interactions at the IEP meeting.

FIGURE 2.13

Tips for Improving Teacher/Parent Interactions

- Make contact with the parents when the student initially enters the classroom.
- Facilitate communication by asking leading questions. (See Figure 2.14, "Parent Interview Questions.")
- Ask how parents want to be involved in their child's progress during the school year.
- Ask if and how parents want to be involved in their child's education.
- Explain to parents the use of the classroom aides: the breakdown of time with students between aides and teachers.

FIGURE 2.14

Parent Interview Questions

1. What would you like your child to learn this year?
2. What means success for your child?
3. What are your (parent) expectations?
4. What are some changes you would like to see for your child by the end of the year?
5. Could you tell me a little about [student's name]'s school experience?
   - Does [student's name] like school?
   - Did s/he go to preschool?
   - When did s/he get involved with special education?
   - At what age was s/he identified? What grade?
   - Do you have any concerns at this time?
   - What works well for you when dealing with the schools?
   - Were there any long absences from school for [student's name?] (Any hospitalizations?)
   - Are there any medical issues that I should be aware of in order to help your child in school?

PREPARING FOR IEP MEETINGS

Before the IEP meeting, you will be expected to interpret the results of the initial evaluation or assessment and prepare a report. The school psychologist will present the results of a psychological evaluation. Prepare your notes for the meeting. You will need an agenda for the meeting and maybe a script. Ask if your school site already has an agenda for you to follow for the meeting. We offer a sample meeting agenda for you to use (Figure 2.15).

A useful preparation practice to do before an IEP meeting is to have a preplanning conversation with the school psychologist, occupational therapist, speech pathologist, or any other member of the IEP team, including the administrator and parent. This conversation allows multiple perspectives to be discussed before the IEP meeting and also helps to clarify the purpose of the IEP meeting.

ENHANCING THE SPECIAL EDUCATION TEACHER'S ROLE AT IEP MEETINGS

The special education teacher plays a critical role during the IEP meeting. We offer the following suggestions to help make your meetings effective, productive, and worthwhile:

- Create a positive setting in the IEP meeting by opening with a positive, hopeful comment about the student.
- Have a clear and open communication with parents.

FIGURE 2.15

Sample IEP Team Agenda

Source: Sample IEP team agenda developed by Laurel Hill-Ward, M.A., California State University—Chico, Chico, CA.

Welcome and Introductions

- Introduce everyone at the meeting and explain their roles.
- Explain the purpose and targeted time frame for the meeting.
- Avoid using the special education "alphabet soup." (Avoid using acronyms.)

Review Procedural Safeguards

- Share assessment results:
  Discuss strengths and needs as documented by data.
  Discuss present level of academic performance, and functional skills.

- Ask for parent's input throughout the meeting (e.g., "Do you also see this at home?").

Determine Special Education Eligibility

- Identify primary disability based on multiple assessment data.

Determine Measurable Annual IEP Goals

Determine Placement

Determine Process to Report Student's Progress to Parent

Ask If There Are Any Questions and Thank Everyone for Attending the Meeting

■ Look at parents as "experts."
■ Report honestly the good and troublesome actions of students.
■ Make positive suggestions for improvement.
■ Be open to trying new ideas.
■ Establish a trusting relationship with parents.
■ Keep notes of the kinds of questions and worries from parents and administrators.
■ Be the person to ask the parents how they feel about what is being suggested in the IEP meeting.
■ Ensure that the parents understand the information before them.
■ Take the pressure off parents by suggesting a short break in high-stress situations.

CREATING EFFECTIVE IEP TEAM MEETINGS

An important part of the IEP meeting is that everyone has an opportunity to be heard, and the special education teacher can help create a climate that fosters this process. A typical IEP meeting takes about 1 hour. Be aware that the length of time needed for the meeting can vary a great deal. We recommend, at the beginning of the meeting, to let the IEP team know what the targeted time frame for the meeting is so that all IEP members can take responsibility for keeping the agenda moving along.

CONCLUSION

The IEP process has been referred to as the "heart" of special education. According to IDEA 2004, the individualized education program (IEP) includes statements of:

1. Present levels of academic achievement and functional performance, including how the disability affects involvement and progress in the general curriculum, or for preschoolers, how disability affects participation in appropriate activities
2. Annual measurable goals and short-term objectives for students who are assessed using alternate achievement standards (annual measurable goals must include academic and functional goals)
3. Special education and related services and supplementary aids and services needed to advance toward annual goals and to be involved and make progress in the general curriculum
4. The extent to which the child will not participate in the general education classroom
5. Modifications needed to participate in assessments, and if an assessment is not appropriate, how the child will be assessed
6. Frequency and location of services and modifications
7. Transition service needs beginning not later than the first IEP in effect when the student is 16 and updated annually, of appropriate measurable postsecondary goals based on age-appropriate transition assessments related to training, education, employment, and, where appropriate, independent skills
8. Information regarding transfer of rights at the age of majority
9. How child's progress will be measured and how parents will be informed

This chapter presents both legal and pragmatic issues related to the IEP process. We caution you regarding issues of student confidentiality, strongly recommending that professional judgment be used when sharing IEP information. Figure 2.16 is a poem about IEPs by an anonymous author. We have included it for your enjoyment as you reflect on the IEP process.

FIGURE 2.16

Dr. Suess's IEP (Uses the rhythm from *Green Eggs and Ham)*

Source: Anonymous.

Do you like these IEPs?

I do not like these IEPs
I do not like them, Geez Louise
We test, we check
We plan, we meet
But nothing ever seems complete

Would you, could you like the form?

I do not like the form I see
Not page 1, not 2, not 3
Another change
A brand new box
I think we all
Have lost our rocks

Could you all meet here or there?

We could not meet here or there
We cannot all fit anywhere!
Not in a room
Not in a hall
There seems to be no space at all

Would you, could you meet again?

I cannot meet again next week
No lunch, no prep
Please hear me speak
No not at dusk. No not at dawn
At 4pm I should be gone

Could you hear while all speak out?
Would you write they words they spout?

I could not hear, I would not write
This does not need to be a fight
Sign here, date there
Mark this, check that
Beware the student's ad-vo-cat (e)
You do not like them
So you say
Try again, try again!
And you may

If you will let me be
I will try again
You'll see

Say!

I almost like these IEPs!
I think I'll write six thousand three
And I will practice day and night
Until they say
"You've got it right!"

EXPLORATIONS

1. Assume your administrator asked you to make a presentation to the staff about special education. What points are important to include? How would you present the information?
2. Think about how each of your students is receiving special education services. Have you considered all possibilities for delivery of services for your students? Meet with your colleagues to discuss ideas and possibly consider a plan that might be more effective for each of your students.
3. Develop a plan to assist parents in understanding special education. If you were the parent in an IEP meeting, how would you like information presented? You might consider creating a Web page, a PowerPoint presentation, an Internet discussion forum, or a workshop based on the parents' needs.
4. What are some questions or concerns you have about IDEA in your school? Engage in a discussion with your colleagues to learn more about providing interventions that will allow your students to experience success.
5. Review the parent interview questions list (Figure 2.14). Select one of your student's parents to interview. What did you learn from the parent responses that you received? How do you plan to incorporate the responses into your student's instructional program or curriculum content?
6. How do you create a climate at the IEP meeting so that everyone has an opportunity to be heard, yet at the same time, the IEP meeting agenda is able to move along at a realistic pace? You may want to discuss this question with other special education teachers and mentors.
7. Develop a plan or checklist based on the information in this chapter to help you prepare for IEP meetings. This way, you will be able to complete those parts you are responsible for in a timely and efficient manner.
8. Add your personal notes to the sample IEP meeting agenda presented in this chapter to help you to remember key points and behaviors during the meeting. Remember: Be honest, be kind, and be necessary!

WEBSITES

California Association of Resource Specialists Plus

http://www.carsplus.org

This site is the CA State Resource Specialist Plus (CARS+) organization site. The organization's sole purpose is to represent the unique needs of resource specialists and other special education teachers. Provides a guide for writing IEP goals and objectives to standards.

Council for Exceptional Children's Summary of Significant Issues in IDEA 2004

http://www.cec.sped.org/pp/IDEA_120204.pdf

IDEA 2004 (PL 108–446)

http://www.copyright.gov/legislation/pl108-446.html#306

Idea Practices

http://www.ideapractices.org

This site provides extensive information on IDEA. Links to articles for teachers as well as information on upcoming conferences is presented.

Individual Education Planning: A Handbook for Developing and Implementing IEPs

http://www.edu.gov.mb.ca/metks4/instruct/specedu/iep/index.html

This Website expands on the information provided in the document, "Individual Education Planning: A Handbook for Developing and Implementing IEPs."

LD Online
http://www.ldonline.org/ld_indepth/iep/seven_habits.html
E. Hammar and A. Malatchi list seven habits of highly effective IEP teams.

National Association of School Psychologists
http://www.nasponline.org/advocacy/IDEAinformation.html

National Association of State Directors of Special Education Website on IDEA
http://www.aph.org/advisory/nasdse.html

National Center for the Dissemination of Disability Research
http://www.ncddr.org/

National Dissemination Center for Children with Disabilities
http://www.nichcy.org/

National Education Association's chart for highly qualified teachers
http://www.nea.org/specialed/images/ideahqtchart.pdf
This site provides an overview chart for determining if a teacher is highly qualified or not.

Special Education Resources on the Internet (SERI)
http://www.seriweb.com
This site is a collection of special education Internet-accessible information resources.

U.S. House of Representatives Report 108–77
http://www.nasponline.org/advocacy/IDEAHouseReport.pdf

U.S. Senate Report 108–105
http://edworkforce.house.gov/issues/108th/education/idea/conferencereport/confrept.htm

Wrights Law on IDEA 2004
http://www.wrightslaw.com/idea/idea.2004.all.pdf

REFERENCES

Center for Applied Special Technology. (2007). Universal design for learning. Retrieved June 9, 2007 from http://www.cast.org/research/edu.

Council for Exceptional Children. (1999). *The IEP team guide*. Reston, VA: Author.

Dabkowski, D. M. (2004). Encouraging active parent participation in IEP team meetings. *Exceptional Children, 36*(3), 34–39.

Drasgow, E., Yell, M. L., & Robinson, T. R. (2001). Developing legally correct and educationally appropriate IEPs. *Remedial and Special Education, 22,* 359–373.

Fuchs, D., & Fuchs, L. S. (2005). Responsiveness to intervention: A blueprint for practitioners, policymakers, and parents. *Teaching Exceptional Children, 38*(1), 57–61.

Fuchs, D., Mock, D., Morgan, P. L., & Young, C. (2003). Responsiveness-to-intervention: Definitions, evidence, and implications for the learning disabilities construct. *Learning Disabilities Research & Practice, 18,* 157–171.

Johns, B. H., Crowley, E. P., & Guetzloe, E. (2002). *Effective curriculum for students with emotional and behavioral disorders.* Denver, CO: Love Publishing Company.

Klinger, J. K., & Edwards, P. A. (2006). *Cultural considerations with response to intervention.* Position statement. National Center for Culturally Responsive Educational Systems (NCCREST).

Mandlawitz, M. (2006). *What every teacher should know about IDEA 2004.* Boston, MA: Allyn & Bacon.

National Association of State Directors of Special Education. (1996). *Enhancing individual student accountability through the IEP: Report of the Wingspread Conference on accountability in special education.* Alexandria, VA: National Association of State Directors of Special Education.

Rock, M. L. (2000). Parents as equal partners: Balancing the scales in IEP development. *Exceptional Children, 32*(6), 30–37.

Rose, D. H., Meyer, A., & Hitchcock, C. (Eds). (2005). *The Universally Designed Classroom:* Accessible curriculum and digital technologies. Cambridge, MA: Harvard Education Press.

Sorrells, A., Rieth, H., & Sindelar, P. (Eds.). (2004). *Critical issues in special education.* Boston, MA: Allyn & Bacon.

Tilley, W. D. (2006). Response to intervention: An overview. What is it? Why do it? Is it worth it? *The Special Edge, 19*(2), 1, 4–5, 10.

U.S. Department of Education. (2003). *Twenty-fourth annual report to Congress on implementation of the Individuals with Disabilities Education Act.* Washington, DC: Author.

Vaughn, S., & Fuchs, L. (2003). Redefining learning disabilities inadequate response to instruction: The promise and potential problem. *Learning Disabilities Research and Practice, 18*(3), 137–146.

Zigmond, N. (2003). Where should students with disabilities receive special education services? Is one place better than another? *Journal of Special Education, 37*, 193–199.

3

Classroom Management and Organization

"It is common sense to take a method and try it. If it fails, admit it frankly and try another. But above all, try something."

Franklin Delano Roosevelt

CHAPTER OBJECTIVES

- ▨ Present practical tips for managing your classroom
- ▨ Provide recommendations for rules/procedures
- ▨ Present steps for reducing classroom disruptions
- ▨ Discuss how to implement a classroom reward system
- ▨ Discuss guidelines for conducting class meetings

> *Before reading this chapter, think about what motivates you to want to learn. What kind of learning environment makes you feel safe and willing to take risks? What is your greatest concern regarding classroom management? Record your reflections and revisit your response as you read this chapter.*

INTRODUCTION

For the purposes of this guide, classroom management refers to the orchestration or operation of your special education classroom or learning environment as a whole. Effective classroom management begins with planning and organization. California Special Education Alternative Certification Project directors Barry Ziff and Andrea Zetlin (2004) recommend that before you start teaching at a new school, you should be familiar with its facilities and resources, understand the philosophy, policies, and calendar for the academic year, and, if possible, send each student an introduction letter.

Many volumes and resources are available on the subject of classroom management for both general and special educators. (For some examples, see the Websites and References sections at the end of this chapter.) To help you get started in the special education setting, the discussion of classroom management for this chapter will focus on the learning environment in terms of arranging the classroom environment, maximizing instructional time, scheduling activities, establishing rules and procedures, reducing classroom interruptions, implementing a reward system, and conducting class meetings. Contributors to this chapter are project faculty from an alternative certification program

FIGURE 3.1

Did You Know?

Source: Ziff & Zetlin, 2004. Reprinted with permission.

Organization and planning are keys to establishing effective classroom management and promoting positive student interactions.

in California respected for their expertise in classroom management. Dr. Barry Ziff and Dr. Andrea Zetlin from California State University, Los Angeles Charter College of Education, Division of Special Education Internship Program have contributed content information to this chapter of the guide (see Figure 3.1).

PRACTICAL TIPS FOR MANAGING YOUR CLASSROOM

ARRANGING THE CLASSROOM ENVIRONMENT

Chairs, desks, bookcases, tables, room dividers, instructional equipment such as computers, and other furniture need to be arranged for safety and ease of use. Materials and file folders used frequently by your students should be kept in designated areas of your classroom and within easy access for both you and your students. Materials used less frequently such as video equipment and art supplies should be stored in closets.

When planning the arrangement of classroom furniture and equipment, it is critical to remember that you must be able to visually see multiple points in the classroom from any one place. The same is true for your students. Regardless of how you arrange the furniture, each student should be able to see the teacher, the paraprofessional, and the chalkboard or white board. This means that the placement of tables, chairs, computer stations, educational support equipment, and room dividers must never block your view of students or your students' view of you. This is both a safety and a monitoring issue.

You should place furniture and seating areas so that you and your students can easily walk to the teacher's desk, the pencil sharpener, and the front door without disturbing other students. Areas with limited distractions can be created with the use of bookcases and filing cabinets. Even in the most limited amount of space, focusing on the structural details and the association of certain spaces with certain activities helps your students to understand the expectations in the learning environment without dependence upon verbal directions or cuing from you. Many classroom management issues can be resolved by attention to the physical learning space.

Although special education learning environments may differ from program to program (self-contained classrooms, resource rooms, learning center models), from grade to grade (elementary, middle school, and high school), and due to students' degrees of disability (learning disabilities, emotional/behavior disorders, physical disabilities, and intellectual impairments), some common elements are needed when arranging the physical learning environments for students with special needs. Regardless of program, grade, or disability there is a need for a common large-group area, an area for small-group instruction, an area for one-on-one instruction, and an area for independent study. These distinct areas give your students a clear message about the type of activities as well as the behavioral expectations associated with each space in the learning environment. A sample floor plan of a special education classroom is presented in Figure 3.2.

When working in the common large-group area your students will feel that they are an important part of a learning community that encourages participation, problem solving, decision making, and contribution as a member of a group or team. Group academic discussions, class meetings, film viewing, and class projects or activities (such as service learning

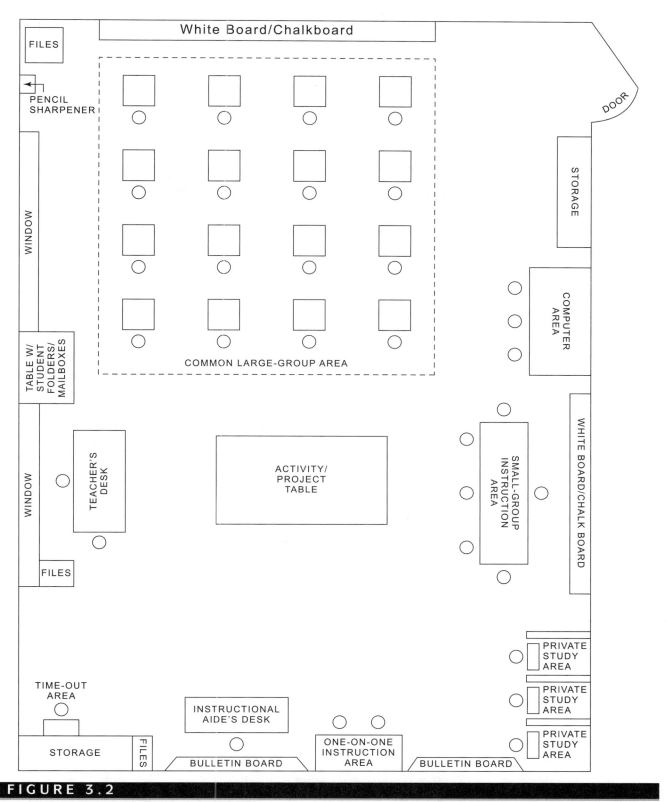

FIGURE 3.2

Sample Special Education Classroom Floor Plan

Source: Rosenberg, Michael S.; O'Shea, Lawrence J.; O'Shea, Dorothy J.; *Student teacher to master teacher: A practical guide for educating students with special needs*, 4th edition, © 2006, p. 62. Adapted by permission of Pearson Education, Inc., Upper Saddle River, NJ.

activities, newspaper production, or book publishing) take place in this large common area. This designated classroom area promotes social interaction and positive group affiliation.

The small-group instruction area is needed for instructional grouping for academic skill building and acquisition of classroom behaviors. The expectation for this smaller learning area is that your students will engage in academic learning time and be responsible for learning new information and skills. This smaller, safer space provides a good practice area for your students to participate in teacher-directed lessons and learn new information and behaviors that are expected in the general education classroom. For example, raising their hands to respond, waiting their turn to answer or ask questions, listening to the teacher and other students, following verbal and written directions, working cooperatively, and not disrupting others are behavioral skills needed for students to succeed in the general education classroom. Practicing these skills during small-group instruction builds good student habits that can carry over into the mainstream classroom. Many times teachers, particularly secondary teachers, assume that all students know these skills. More typically than not, it is the students' lack of knowledge and confidence about these skills that leads to problems in classroom management and results in school discipline actions.

The location of the one-on-one instruction area within the larger learning space is critical when designing the physical space of your special education learning environment. In this area students are expected to focus on themselves and their own learning curve. It is a private space that permits risk taking and a safe place for making mistakes without fear of criticism or laughter by other students. This space is used by you and your paraprofessional to provide one-on-one instruction to your students. When your students are in this area the conversation remains between the instructor and the student, not with other students seated in other areas of the room. If your students understand this, then you have created a safe, quiet learning environment for tackling new information and skills. When your students are ready to do independent work, they need to move to another designated area.

An area for independent work helps to build your students' self-confidence and capability toward learning. Learning in the best sense is a lifelong and self-initiated endeavor. When you provide independent study space for your students, you are giving them the message that you respect them and their ability to learn and work by themselves. Too many times, teachers assume that their special education students cannot do this. Providing a safe, structured environment for independent study or exploration, regardless of your students' age or disability, permits your students to become comfortable with themselves and their individual learning process.

You can create a physical space where your students feel a sense of pride and belonging by displaying their work in an attractive manner and constructing age-appropriate bulletin boards.

Figure 3.3 provides a checklist for arranging the classroom environment, and Figure 3.4 asks you to reflect on this aspect of your teaching.

MAXIMIZING INSTRUCTIONAL TIME

Research points out the direct relationship between engaged time on task and higher levels of student achievement (Winn, Menlove, & Zsiray, 1997). Johns, Crowley, and Guetzloe (2002) believe that the most important goal for you, as the teacher, is to provide a high degree of engaged time, defined as time spent doing meaningful activities that are based on each student's specific learning needs. These authors agree that too much "downtime" occurs during a school day. Thus, to increase the amount of engaged

FIGURE 3.3

Checklist for
Arranging the
Classroom
Environment

Source: Developed by
Dr. Barry Ziff and
Dr. Andrea Zetlin, 2004.

When setting up your classroom, is your classroom arranged:

- To facilitate learning? _____

- To promote orderly movement? _____

- To minimize distractions and noise? _____

- To improve the quality of student interaction? _____

- To increase time on task? _____

- To best monitor student work and behavior? _____

- To allow for easy access to materials? _____

- To keep high-traffic areas free from congestion? _____

- To be sure teacher can see all students? _____

- To allow all students visible access to presentations and displays? _____

FIGURE 3.4

Take a Moment

Think About	Reflect	Respond
The arrangement of your classroom or learning environment	Look around the classroom. How does the room arrangement address safety and accessibility issues? How could you improve the design of this learning environment?	

time, researchers (Johns et al., 2002; Montague, Bergeron, & Lago-Delello, 1997; Stewart, Evans, and Kaczynski, 1997) suggest the following:

- Provide a signal for transitions. Transitions refer to the times when your students change activities, classrooms, or subjects. Use a bell, music, lights, arm gesture, or phrase to signal transitions. Many special education students have a difficult time adapting to change, especially during unstructured or non-teacher-directed time. To minimize problems that can occur during transitions times, you need to reward appropriate responses often and provide immediate consequences when necessary (Maroney, 2004; Ziff & Zetlin, 2004). You can also create teacher-imposed structures for your students such as carrying "travel packs" filled with learning activities that they can complete without assistance upon arriving at another classroom or work area within your classroom. It is important to provide opportunities for your students to practice each transition so that eventually routines begin to emerge (Ziff & Zetlin, 2004).

- Schedule learning activities properly and make sure that the work required by the task is appropriate for the time allotted. It is a good idea to always have back-up plans such as extra credit or bonus work or a special learning center or computer program. For those students who finish early, any independent activity must be related to the skill that you are currently teaching.

- Plan and select engaged-time activities that provide your students with a high level of success.

■ Ask yourself, "What is the reason for learning this?" and "What is the relevance for this particular student?" for any worksheet or group lesson that you give to your students.
■ Give clear, precise directions to your students before assigning a task.
■ Monitor your students' progress by providing frequent, positive reinforcement and corrective feedback.
■ Reward and recognize your students for completing tasks.
■ Analyze your use of academic and nonacademic time in the classroom.

To help you plan your instructional time, the suggested time frame for a 1-hour lesson in reading, math, science, or language arts according to Ziff and Zetlin (2004) is:

■ 3–5 minutes for motivation/introduction
■ 15 minutes for teacher-led group lesson
■ 5–7 minutes for closure
■ 5 minutes for transition

Use Figure 3.5 to reflect on your instructional planning and students' engaged time.

SCHEDULING ACTIVITIES

When scheduling activities for your special education program, it is important to develop a schedule of relatively consistent daily tasks. To organize your program, you will need to develop and implement a master program schedule.

The master schedule is simply an overall class schedule. The following information is included on the master schedule:

■ When? The beginning and ending time for each period of instruction
■ What? The subject area or activity to be covered (indicate whether it is a general education class activity or a related service)
■ Who? The adult responsible for leading or supervising the period
■ Where? The location where the activity needs to be completed

A visual representation of the master schedule is shown in Figure 3.6. The master schedule should be large enough to be easily read when posted in the classroom.

When figuring out your master schedule, the teacher's activity time is considered as well as your students' learning goals as identified in their IEPs. Using the example of the master class schedule in Figure 3.6, it is apparent that during Period 1, Mr. Lot, the

---

FIGURE 3.5

Take a Moment

Think About	Reflect	Respond
Your instructional activities in relation to engaged time	Divide the teaching day into 15-minute segments and list the activities that reflect successful engaged time next to the appropriate time slot. If you do this for at least five days, a pattern will emerge. Based on this information, how can you improve the scheduling of learning activities.	

Name of Student	Period 1 Time:	Period 2 Time:	Period 3 Time:	Period 4 Time:	Period 5 Time:	Period 6 Time:	Period 7 Time:
Sally	Reading w/Mr. Lot at reading table	Art class w/Ms. Lee Room 101 Gen. Ed.	Math w/Mr. Lot at math table	Lunch	Writing center w/Mr. Lot at writing center table	Spelling w/Mr. Lot at reading table	Social studies w/Mr. Gray Room 103 Gen. Ed.
Michael	Reading w/Mr. Lot at reading table	Spelling w/Mr. Lot at reading table	Math w/Mr. Lot at math table	Lunch	Writing center w/Mr. Lot at writing center table	Social studies w/Mr. Gray Room 103 Gen Ed.	Computer skills w/Ms. Lane Room 405 Gen. Ed.
Joshua	Reading w/Mr. Lot at reading table	Speech w/Ms. Sal Room 45 Related Service	Math w/Mr. Lot at math table	Lunch	Writing Center w/Mr. Lot at writing center table	Spelling w/Mr. Lot at reading table	Social studies w/Mr. Gray Room 103 Gen. Ed.
Maria	Reading w/Mr. Lot at reading table	Spelling w/Mr. Lot at reading table	Math w/Mr. Lot at math table	Lunch	Writing center w/Mr.Lot at writing center table	Social studies w/Mr. Gray Room 103 Gen Ed.	Computer skills w/Ms. Lane Room 405 Gen. Ed.

FIGURE 3.6

Sample Master Schedule

special educator, is teaching reading. During Period 2, Mr. Lot is teaching spelling. In Period 3, Mr. Lot is teaching math. During Period 4, it would make sense for Mr. Lot to take his lunch break, since he doesn't have any students at this time. During Period 5, he is teaching writing; and in Period 6, Mr. Lot is teaching spelling. During Period 7, Mr. Lot is not providing direct instruction to students; so during this time frame, Mr. Lot may use the time to co-teach in the general education classroom, assess students, work on IEP paperwork, and contact families, administrators, or general education teachers.

From the master class schedule, individual schedules can be created to help your students remember their own activities each day. The schedules can be printed at a small size and carried by your students or, if needed, taped to their desks.

FLEXIBLE GROUPING

Dr. Barry Ziff and Dr. Andrea Zetlin (2004) recommend a flexible grouping approach based on your students' needs, interests, and abilities to maximize instructional time. The three types of learning activities are: T = directed lesson (teacher directed), F = follow-up activities (independent seatwork), and EN = enrichment activities (interest centers,

FIGURE 3.7

Flexible Grouping
Matrix

Source: Ziff & Zetlin,
2004. Reprinted with
permission

Top Group	Low Group	Middle Group
T	EN	F
F	T	EN
EN	F	T

Three types of learning activities are:
- T = Directed lesson (teacher directed)
- F = Follow-up activities (independent work)
- EN = Enrichment activities (interest centers, individual projects)

FIGURE 3.8

Take a Moment

Think About	Reflect	Respond
Scheduling activities	Is the activity schedule efficient? Does the scheduling of activities address individual learning needs and maximize instructional time? How can you rearrange the schedule to accommodate different learning abilities and types of learning activities?	

individual projects). Dr. Ziff offers a matrix (Figure 3.7) to help you structure your classroom instructional activities and schedule. For example, when you are providing direct instruction to your students with higher abilities, your students with lower-level skills are engaged in enrichment activities that do not require your immediate attention, and your groups of students who have middle-level abilities are completing independent work. The matrix provides a way to structure your classroom to meet the learning needs of all of your students and manage your time to ensure that your students engage in all three types of activities. Figure 3.8 will help you reflect on your use of flexible grouping.

ESTABLISHING RULES AND PROCEDURES

Rules inform your students about what is acceptable behavior in the special education setting. Some special education teachers choose to establish rules collaboratively with their students, whereas others prefer to create a list of rules and post them in the classroom, so that they are clearly visible on the first day of school. Guidelines for establishing class rules are provided in Figure 3.9.

Procedures explain how to appropriately complete a task or activity. Rules and procedures provide structure and communicate behavioral standards and expectations. So, it is critical that the rules are clear and understandable by your students. Furthermore, the classroom rules and procedures must align with your particular school's expectations of student behavior. When developing rules and procedures, the following guidelines are offered:

1. Know your school district policies regarding rules and discipline procedures.
2. Discuss, develop, and review the classroom rules and procedures on the first day of school.

FIGURE 3.9

Establishing Rules

Source: Ziff & Zetlin, 2004. Reprinted with permission.

Guidelines for Establishing Rules
- Few in number
- Need to be explicit, simple, and direct
- Word rules positively
- Students participate in making rules
- Post rules
- Follow rules consistently
- Teach rules to students

Examples of Effective Rules
- Follow directions
- Act responsibly
- Work quietly
- Be prepared
- Keep your hands to yourself
- Be considerate to others
- Have pride in your work

Best Three Rules for Classroom Management
- Take responsibility for yourself
- Have pride in your work
- Respect yourself and others

3. Keep the number of classroom rules and procedures small.
4. Post your rules and procedures clearly in the learning environment.
5. Allow the students to practice the rules.
6. Continue to focus on the basic procedures through discussions, reviews, and rehearsals.
7. Explain the location of the bathrooms, library, and offices, as well as where to line up for buses, recess, lunch, and so on.
8. Hand out all books and materials in an orderly fashion.
9. Build a daily routine/pattern.
10. Explain where all materials and resources can be found.
11. Practice all activities to establish a routine.

Explicit and consistent procedures will create an organized and safe learning environment for your students with special needs. For example, when procedures are developed for routine tasks such as morning arrival, daily attendance, collection of lunch money, walking to and from the classroom, turning in homework, and beginning and ending instructional time, your students will feel secure and more relaxed, and thus ready to learn. Without these routines in place, your students will be demonstrating off-task behaviors and you will be spending the majority of your teaching time dealing with classroom and behavior management issues rather than providing instruction for engaged academic learning. Figure 3.10 offers a checklist for establishing classroom routines.

REDUCING CLASSROOM DISRUPTIONS

Careful planning and organization contribute to building a successful learning environment. The following steps prevent classroom disruptions (Ziff & Zetlin, 2004):

■ Create an effective design for physical space.
■ Follow a daily schedule.

FIGURE 3.10
Checklist for
Establishing Routines
Source: Ziff & Zetlin,
2004. Reprinted with
permission.

An important aspect of an effective and successful classroom is establishing procedures for all activities. All procedures and rules must be specifically taught through structured lessons to establish routines for each of the following:

- beginning-the-day activities
- entering and exiting the classroom
- transitioning from one activity to another
- sharpening a pencil
- distributing supplies and materials
- asking for assistance
- participating in a discussion
- ending-the-day activities
- handing in assignments
- fire, tornado or earthquake drills

- Maintain comprehensive lesson plans.
- Develop and teach rules and procedures.
- Continually monitor and enforce rules.
- Monitor classroom for potentially disruptive behavior.
- Reinforce appropriate behavior.
- Respond quickly and firmly to disruptive behavior.
- Maintain a sense of humor.
- Be consistent in following a classroom management plan.
- Ask for help when necessary.

IMPLEMENTING A CLASSROOM REWARD SYSTEM

It is critical to develop a management plan that is appropriate for the maturational age of your students. A classroom reward system may be appropriate and helpful in creating a calm, structured, and organized learning environment. To plan and implement a reward system you need to identify target behaviors, identify reinforcers, establish a system, inform students, develop a plan to fade the rewards, and establish a clear record-keeping system. For your system to be successful, you need to explain the plan to parents and administrators in addition to your students, and establish procedures for noncompliant students from the beginning. Fading the reward system can be accomplished by providing more social rewards, delaying reinforcement, and teaching self-management (Ziff & Zetlin, 2004). Figure 3.11 provides an opportunity for you to reflect on creating a safe and organized learning environment.

CONDUCTING CLASS MEETINGS

Class meetings provide empowering opportunities for your students to gain practice and skills with interpersonal communications, as well as collaboratively problem solve individual issues and classroom concerns. According to Paul Zionts and Richard W. Fox (1998, p. 8), "The development and nurturing of empathy, acceptance, and group support are natural outcomes of group experiences." The following guidelines adapted from Zionts and Fox (1998) for class meetings will help you to get started implementing this classroom management technique:

1. Develop specific goals and objectives for class meetings.
2. Review rules of the classroom out loud.

FIGURE 3.11

Take a Moment

Think About	Reflect	Respond
Establishing an organized and safe learning environment	Are there explicit and consistent procedures in the classroom that create an organized and safe learning environment? What are these procedures? What routines would you put in place to reduce off-task behaviors?	

3. Establish special rules for class meetings:
   - Students must respect peers.
   - Participation is voluntary at all times.
4. Consider size of group, amount of time for discussion, and physical arrangement of group (horseshoe and circle are preferred).
5. Build trust by starting and ending on time, listen carefully to your students, follow the intervention you have chosen, and remain calm, consistent, and fair when handling behavioral disruptions.
6. Honor the cultural and ethnic norms of your students.
7. Approach the first meeting as an ice-breaker, where students share their names and tell something about themselves.
8. Review vocabulary words for meetings.
9. Listen actively.
10. Reflect thoughts, perceptions, and feelings.
11. Seek clarification and use questioning strategies.
12. Summarize concisely and give mini-lectures ("sound bites").
13. Communicate encouragement and support.

CREATING A CLASSROOM COMMUNITY

When students with special needs feel that they are valued and respected, especially within a group setting, their self-esteem improves. A classroom environment that is welcoming, caring, respectful of individual differences, and where each student feels safe is a place where your students will want to spend their time and learn. Building a classroom community fosters such an environment and supports relationships between students. Practical steps for creating a classroom community include the following:

■ Make sure that everyone in the classroom knows each other's name and shares at least one area of interest or hobby with each other. When sharing names and areas of interest, be sure that all students are listening to each other and are respectful of each other's time to share.

■ Assign an appropriate task or responsibility that is relevant and meaningful for each student in your class. An appropriate task is defined as one that your student can perform successfully without assistance. This task needs to be relevant, meaningful, and beneficial to the class as a whole. Passing out student folders, reading announcements, watering classroom plants, and erasing the board in preparation for the next lesson are examples of beneficial tasks.

■ Model respect, concern, and politeness for your students and require that your students treat each other in the same manner.

■ Create a joint productive activity that tells your students that they are valued and that they can be successful as a learner, classmate, and friend. Introducing a class project where students need to work together to create something to share with others promotes a sense of community. Examples of joint productive activities are the production of a class newspaper, a class yearbook, a class manual or book, or a puppet show on a "hot topic" or theme that teaches a lesson. A service learning project, described further in Chapter 7, is another method for building classroom community while simultaneously addressing the self-confidence and self-esteem of your students.

In essence, you are building a "team" of students who know about each other, care about each other, and have the abilities and skills to work together to produce something that is beneficial to the group as a whole. Your role as teacher in this community is one of coach, model, and participant member.

CONCLUSION

Organization and planning are keys to managing a learning environment that promotes positive student interactions and increased academic engaged time. This chapter presents practical recommendations for arranging the classroom environment, maximizing instructional time, scheduling activities, establishing rules and procedures, reducing classroom interruptions, implementing a classroom reward system, and conducting class meetings. The next chapter will focus on individual behavior management.

EXPLORATIONS

1. Before school begins, learn about your school's philosophy, facilities, resources, policies, and calendar. How can you learn this information? Is this information available in print or electronically? Whom can you ask? Once you have acquired this information, create a school resource binder and place copies of your school's attendance policy, discipline policy, and academic yearly calendar in your binder for future reference.

2. Create a diagram of your classroom and analyze it based on the information in this chapter to structure your classroom for success. How could you rearrange your classroom to maximize instructional time and reduce classroom interruptions?

3. Review the section in this chapter on rules and procedures. Compare the guidelines and examples for establishing rules and procedures in this chapter with the rules and procedures in your classroom. How can you create rules and procedures that will improve your classroom management?

4. Review the chapter sections on implementing a classroom reward system and conducting class meetings. Would either of these techniques work for you? Why or why not? If you have never used a reward system or conducted a class meeting, you may want to try these classroom management approaches and critically assess the results.

WEBSITES

CAFS (Center for Adolescent and Family Studies)—About Us

http://education.indiana.edu/cas/tt/v1i2/what.html

This site has a questionnaire for determining your classroom management profile: authoritarian style, authoritative style, laissez-faire style, or indifferent style.

Classroom Management

http://www.theteachersguide.com/ClassManagement.htm

This site has articles, Internet sites, discussion groups, printouts, and information on books about behavior management.

Classroom Management—School Environment (California Department of Education)

http://www.cde.ca.gov/ls/ss/se/classroommgmt.asp

This California Department of Education site provides a California Resource Guide for Classroom Management that contains chapters on: preventing problem behavior, classroom organization and management, reinforcers, activities for creating a positive learning environment, teaching social skills, instructional strategies, communicating with parents/caregivers, behavioral assessment and related interventions, aggressive behaviors, and other problem behaviors.

Positive Environments, Network of Trainers (PENT)

http://www.pent.ca.gov

This site contains information, suggestions, and strategies for positive environments and supports and provides links to other Websites on behavior management.

REFERENCES

Carpenter, S., & McKee-Higgins, E. (1996). Behavior management in inclusive classrooms, *Remedial and Special Education, 17*(4), 195–203.

Cipani, E. (2004). *Classroom management for all teachers: Twelve plans for evidence-based practice.* Reston, VA: Council for Exceptional Children.

Johns, B. H., Crowley, E. P., & Guetzloe, E. (2002). *Effective curriculum for students with emotional and behavioral disorders.* Denver, CO: Love Publishing Company.

Jones, V. F., & Jones, L. S. (2001). *Comprehensive classroom management: Creating communities of support and solving problems.* Boston: Allyn & Bacon.

Kyle, P. B., & Rogien, L. R. (2003). *Opportunities and options in classroom management.* Boston: Pearson Education.

Lickona, T. (1997). Creating the just community with children. *Theory into Practice, 16*, 97–104.

Maroney, S. A. (2004). Transitions: Increasing the odds for successful transitions. *Beyond Behavior, 13*(3), 29–31.

Montague, M., Bergeron, J., & Lago-Delello, E. (1997). Using prevention strategies in general education. *Focus on Exceptional Children, 29*(8), 1–12.

Rosenberg, M. S., O'Shea, L., & O'Shea, D. J. (2006). *Student teacher to master teacher: A practical guide for educating students with special needs* (4th ed.). Upper Saddle River, NJ: Merrill/Prentice Hall.

Stewart, S., Evans, W., & Kaczynski, D. (1997). Setting the stage for success: Assessing the instructional environment. *Preventing School Failure, 41*(2), 53–56.

Thompson, C. L., & Rudolph, L. B. (1996). *Counseling children* (8th ed.). Pacific Grove, CA: Brooks/Cole.

Williams, P. A., Alley, R. D., & Henson, K. T. (1999). *Managing secondary classrooms: Principles and strategies for effective management and instruction.* Boston, MA: Allyn & Bacon.

Winn, D., Menlove, R., & Zsiray, S. (1997). *Rethinking the scheduling of school time.* Bloomington, IN: Phi Delta Kappa Educational Foundation.

Ziff, B., & Zetlin, A. (2004). California State University Los Angles Education Specialist Intern Program Handbook. Los Angles, CA.

Zionts, P., & Fox, R. W. (1998). Facilitating group classroom meetings: Practical guidelines. *Beyond Behavior, 9,* 8–13.

4

Individual Behavior Management

"The job of an educator is to teach students to see the vitality in themselves."

Joseph Campbell

CHAPTER OBJECTIVES

■ Review theoretical perspectives on behavior
■ Describe the positive behavior support process
■ Discuss applicable interventions

Before reading this chapter, think about what comes to mind when teaching students who demonstrate challenging behaviors. When does the inappropriate social behavior occur? What triggers the behavior? What are some of your ideas for dealing with the behavior? Record your reflections and revisit your response as you read this chapter.

INTRODUCTION

Behavior management poses the most difficult challenges for all teachers, and especially for special education teachers. Working with students who have learning difficulties in addition to other problems in school and at home definitely makes teaching special education students extremely intense at times. Many of the inappropriate behaviors that special education students demonstrate stem from a lack of communication skills and/or a lack of understanding about the interactions involved with building and maintaining interpersonal relationships. Understanding the communicative intent and the motivation variables that sustain certain behaviors will help you to realize why you may choose to use one behavioral management technique in favor of another.

This chapter provides definitions and descriptions of behavior management terms, processes, and interventions commonly used in special education to provide you with an overview of individual behavior management and supplement the information presented in your core program.

THEORETICAL PERSPECTIVES

Researchers and educators refer to major theoretical perspectives or conceptual models that provide an explanation for problem behaviors and general approaches to interventions derived from each perspective. These theoretical perspectives or models are: psychodynamic, biophysical, psycho-educational, ecological, humanistic, behavioral, and cognitive learning. Gaining an awareness of the theoretical perspectives will help you to learn about the major approaches to behavior management and why multiple interventions exist. To help you understand, we have adapted a chart from Dice (1994). Figure 4.1 provides an overview of the major theoretical perspectives, an explanation for the inappropriate behavior based on this perspective, and interventions typically associated with each perspective. A brief discussion of these perspectives follows.

It is more appropriate for a psychiatrist, psychologist, or medical doctor rather than the classroom teacher to use some of the theoretical models and interventions presented by Dice. However, these interventions impact today's students and their classroom behaviors. Specifically, psychodynamic, biophysical, and psycho-educational approaches are more commonly found in a therapeutic or medical setting than a classroom setting. Ecological, humanistic, behavioral, and cognitive learning perspectives are easily applied and used by the teacher within the classroom setting.

PSYCHODYNAMIC PERSPECTIVE

The psychodynamic model is based on the work of Sigmund Freud. This model applies a medical disease approach to personality and defines deviance as intra-psychic conflict, or as a lack of integration among the mental structures of the mind (id, ego, superego). Applying this model to the classroom results in interventions that include a more permissive environment and the use of role play, drama, drawing, painting, puppets, and physical activities. These interventions help the student gain a greater understanding of his or her feelings and behavior and also provide a nonthreatening activity in which the student may experience some personal success.

PSYCHO-EDUCATIONAL PERSPECTIVE

The psycho-educational model combines the intra-psychic or underlying conflicts with the pressures of functioning in the home, school, and community. This model also posits that insight can lead to changes in behavior. Thus, if the student can identify problems and plan solutions through therapeutic discussion, then the behaviors will change to help him or her adapt to daily pressures. With this intervention, the emphasis is on problem identification and solution planning through one-on-one therapeutic discussion. A technique that applies this perspective directly to problems in everyday classroom interactions is life-space interviewing (LSI). This technique was originally designed for use by teachers in crisis situations, but can be used effectively within a classroom. Teachers must have supervised training to learn appropriate use of LSI.

BIOPHYSICAL PERSPECTIVE

The biophysical model is based on the assumption that human behavior and physiology are connected. Thus, interventions such as surgery, diet control, biofeedback, physical exercise, and drug therapy are used to modify students' learning and behavior. The use of drug therapy, including psychopharmacology, impacts today's classrooms on a widespread basis. As a teacher, it is important to know if your students are receiving any drug therapy

Theoretical Perspective	Reason for Problem Behavior	Major Principles	Interventions
Psychodynamic	Intrapsychic conflict Lack of integration among the mental structures of the mind (id, ego, superego)	Mental structures Catharsis Defense mechanisms Stages of development	Permissive environment Role play, drama drawing, painting, puppetry, physical activities
Biophysical	Defect of anatomy, physiology, neurophysiology	Human behavior and physiology connected	Surgery Diet control Biofeedback Drug therapy Physical exercise
Psycho-educational	Unconscious motivation in combination with pressures of functioning in the home, school, and community	Insight leads to behavior change	Therapeutic discussion Identify problems Plan solution Life-space interview
Ecological	Lack of fit between person and environment	Individual is inseparable part of social system Interactions are reciprocal Influence is bidirectional	Developing skills Adjusting class expectations and/or the classrook environment
Humanistic	Incongruence between the way that an individual views himself and his experience—inner experience such as feelings and emotions or outer experience such as activities or interests	Self-actualization Self-direction Self-fulfillment Free choice leads to a fully functioning person who is open to experience able to trust his or her own judgments, and able to live in the moment, yet redesign oneself based on experience	Relationship between teacher and student Teacher is non-authoritarian resource or catylst for learning, empathetic, nonjudgmental, open, nontraditional, personal Supportive, nurturing, loving environment
Behavioral	Learned problem behaviors	Respondent conditioning Classical or operant conditioning Three-term contingency (ABC) Scientific method	Measurement Evaluation Behavior modification techniques such as positive and negative reinforcers, shaping, scheduling, chaining, fading, punishment (continued)

FIGURE 4.1

Overview of Major Theoretical Perspectives

Source: From *Intervention Strategies for Children with Emotional or Behavioral Disorders* 1st edition by Dice (1994). Reprinted with permission of Wadsworth a division of Thomson Learning: *www.thomsonrights.com* Fax 800-730-2215.

Theoretical Perspective	Reason for Problem Behavior	Major Principles	Interventions
Cognitive Learning	Irritational thinking or self-talk Immature beliefs Errors of cognition	Perception and thinking influence behavior Individuals are largely responsible for creating their own problem behavior	Cognitive social training, self-talk, learn new social behavioral skills Rational-emotive therapy Cognitive social problem solving Cognitive self-monitoring Cognitive self-instruction

FIGURE 4.1
(continued)

and the physical, emotional, and mental impact the drugs may have on your students' behavior and learning ability. This includes students with diabetes who may be insulin users, as well as students taking medications for seizures, attention deficit disorder (ADD), attention deficit hyperactivity disorder (ADHD), obsessive compulsive disorder (OCD), bipolar disorder, asthma, schizophrenia, and depression. If you are uncertain whether a student is taking a medication, check with your school nurse or psychologist. Although medication information may be noted in the student's cumulative file on a health report, or found in the IEP, sometimes this information is not included or easily available.

ECOLOGICAL PERSPECTIVE

Interventions based on an ecological perspective include adjusting class expectations and emphasizing the development of skills. Within this perspective, the problem behavior arises due to a lack of "fit" between the person and the environment. The "problem" behavior does not reside solely in the student, but the problem lies in the relationship between the person and the environment. Thus, a reciprocal relationship exists. Interventions that exemplify this perspective include a teacher helping a student to acquire the needed skills to succeed within the classroom environment or the adjustment of teacher expectations and/or the classroom environment. If an assignment is modified in the general education classroom to accommodate a student with special needs, this is an example of an ecological intervention applied directly to the classroom.

HUMANISTIC PERSPECTIVE

Research has documented the relationship between the quality of teacher-student relationships and the percentage of discipline problems, rule violations, and related problems (Marzano & Marzano, 2003). The Love and Logic Process developed in the mid-1990s by Jim Fay is based on a humanistic perspective to behavioral change and highlights four premises: (1) shared control (you gain control by giving away the control that you don't need), (2) shared thinking and decision making (you provide opportunities for your students to do the greatest amount of thinking and decision making about their behavior), (3) equal shares of empathy with consequences (you avoid anger, threats, warnings or lectures—an absence of anger causes your students to think and learn from their mistakes), and (4) maintenance of your students' self-concepts (you provide empathy and compassion with firm limits and enforceable statements that maintain your students' self-concepts—increased self-concept leads to improved behavior and achievement). The two basic rules of Love and Logic exemplify a humanistic approach promoting self-actualization and competence for students. Simply put, the first rule is: Adults take care of themselves by providing limits in a loving way. The second rule is: Childhood misbehavior is treated as an opportunity for gaining wisdom. Thus, the teacher's role in this behavioral intervention is nonauthoritarian, empathetic, and nonjudgmental.

A major key to this intervention is the relationships that teachers build with their students by establishing and maintaining support. Adapted from Owens and Dieker (2003), the following eight strategies will help you to develop rapport with your students:

1. Greet your students by name inside and outside of the classroom.
2. Recognize special events in your students' lives, such as birthdays, and accomplishments such as an art or service award.
3. Demonstrate kindness to your students, either verbally or with a small note or card.
4. Compliment your students; let them know how nice they look or how well they did on a specific task or activity.
5. Talk to your students about topics that interest them and share your own interests with them.
6. Provide emotional support and encouragement.
7. Spend informal time with your students, and show interest in their personal lives.
8. Create opportunities for students to be involved in activities in which they excel.

BEHAVIORAL PERSPECTIVE

Behavior modification exemplifies a traditional behavioral perspective. The outcome of this intervention is to measurably change or shape a behavior, and the behavioral intervention is not concerned with why the behavior is occurring. This type of intervention analyzes behavior by applying the scientific method of measurement and analysis in terms of a "three-term contingency"—the antecedent (A), the behavior (B), and the consequence (C) (Dice, 1994). This is sometimes referred to as the A-B-C model. Antecedents are environmental stimuli or conditions that occur just prior to a behavior. Consequences are events that occur just after a behavior. The application of consistent consequences is critical for effective behavioral change. Ziff and Zetlin (2004) outline recommendations for providing consistent consequences (see Figure 4.2).

Reinforcers are consequences that strengthen the response that they follow. As a teacher you can provide positive reinforcers to increase appropriate student behaviors and reduce or eliminate problem behaviors. Positive reinforcers can include social recognition such as praise, activities such as privileges and special assignments, and tangible rewards such as tokens, objects, or points.

COGNITIVE LEARNING PERSPECTIVE

This perspective explains problem behavior resulting from "immature beliefs, irrational self-talk, or self-perceptions, and insufficient self-instruction or self-reinforcement" (Dice, 1993, p.74). Students assume responsibility for their own behavior and actions (Hammill & Bartel, 2004). Self-management intervention strategies exemplify a cognitive

FIGURE 4.2

Recommendations
for Providing
Consistent
Consequences

Source: Ziff & Zetlin,
2004. Reprinted with
permission.

- Acknowledge the student's inappropriate behavior.

- Provide a warning.

- Provide positive reinforcement for on-task behavior.

- Provide points to individuals or groups.

- Speak privately with the noncompliant student.

- Provide a loss of privileges.

- Have the student owe time during student nonacademic time.

- Call the student's home.

- Refer the student to the office.

- Consider suspension for serious offenses.

- Provide an individual behavior contract.

- Develop a positive behavior support plan with the IEP team.

learning perspective and actively involve students in monitoring and changing their own behaviors (Salend & Syvestre, 2005). They help your students to gain awareness of their own behaviors and how they affect other classmates. Self-management interventions help students begin to take responsibility for their own behaviors and foster greater independence toward this process. Thus, they are particularly useful for middle and secondary school students. The following activities are examples of self-monitoring strategies (Salend & Syvestre, 2005):

- Self-monitoring: students record their own behaviors on a chart or with the use of computer graphics.
- Self-assessment or self-evaluation: students assess their own behaviors using a checklist or rating scale.
- Self-reinforcement: students are taught to evaluate their own behaviors and then give themselves self-selected rewards, if appropriate.
- Self-instruction: students "self-talk" or verbalize to themselves the responses to the following questions:
    1. "What do I need to do?" (Identify the problem)
    2. "How can I do it?" (Brainstorm potential solutions)
    3. "What is the best way to do it?" (Evaluate solutions)
    4. "Did I do it?" (Use appropriate solutions)
    5. "Does it work?" (Evaluate solutions)

Self-Science is a curriculum program that promotes social and emotional intelligence based on cognitive learning interventions that emphasize student responsibility. Information on this program can be found in the Websites section at the end of this chapter.

DIFFERING PERSPECTIVES

Sometimes individuals (parents, teachers, paraprofessionals, administrators) may disagree on what they believe is the correct approach to behavior management. It is important to realize that this disagreement can stem from differing theoretical perspectives. Therefore, having an understanding of these perspectives or models and their associated interventions

FIGURE 4.3

Did You Know?

Source: Adapted from Van Haren & Fiedler, 2004.

- 85–95% of all students in school have a minimum risk of engaging in violence. Recommendation: Behavior management programs that guide and shape positive behavior in school.

- 5–15% of all students in school are students at risk. Recommendation: Individualized interventions that target specific needs and foster success and positive behavior in school.

- 1–7% of all students in school have intense or chronic behavior problems. Recommendation: Intense individualized support and behavior management in order to be a part of the school environment. Plans and resources to manage difficult crisis situations need to be in place.

can help you to communicate and collaborate more effectively, as well as select an approach that best meets the needs of your students with special needs. Theoretical perspectives and interventions may differ; however, federal special education regulations clearly state that the individualized education program team shall "in the case of a child whose behavior impedes his or her learning or that of others, consider the use of positive behavioral interventions and supports, and other strategies to address that behavior" (34CFR300.324[a][2][i]). See Figure 4.3 for further behavioral recommendations. The next sections of this chapter briefly define and discuss the positive behavior support process.

POSITIVE BEHAVIOR SUPPORT PROCESS

Positive behavior support is a general term in federal regulations that refers to the culturally appropriate application of positive behavioral interventions and systems to achieve socially important behavior change (U.S. Department of Education, 2000). This approach is in contrast to a traditional behavior modification approach because it focuses on *why* the behavior is occurring, or its communicative intent or function. Typically, a behavior modification approach is not concerned with why a problem behavior is occurring, but with the modification of the behavior using either punishments to diminish it or reinforcers to suppress it. In order to determine appropriate, positive behavioral interventions, a functional behavior assessment (FBA) is first conducted and then a positive behavioral support plan is written. This plan identifies behavioral interventions and specifically why, when, and where they will be used. The first step in this process requires a specific description of the behavior. Figure 4.4 asks you to think about an inappropriate behavior and how you would describe it.

FUNCTIONAL BEHAVIOR ASSESSMENT

The function of a behavior is defined as the communicative intent of the behavior. In other words, what is your student getting, protesting, escaping, or avoiding with the behavior? A functional behavior assessment (FBA), as described in federal law, is a systematic process of identifying problem behaviors and the events that reliably predict occurrence and nonoccurrence of those behaviors and maintain the behaviors across time (U.S. Department of Education, 2000). The functional behavior assessment may include a review of records, interviews, and observations to analyze, retrospectively, the function of a specific problem behavior that has occurred at least once (Wright & Gurman, 2001).

FIGURE 4.4
Take a Moment

Think About	Reflect	Respond
A student who demonstrates inappropriate social behavior in the classroom	Describe the behavior that you perceive as inappropriate in very specific, observable terms so that another teacher would be able to recognize it from your description. What does the behavior look like?	

FEDERAL COMPONENTS OF A POSITIVE BEHAVIOR SUPPORT PLAN

Whenever a special education student exhibits behaviors that impede his or her learning or the learning of others, the IEP team must address the situation in the form of a positive behavior support plan according to federal law. The law indicates that the plan provides a summary of interventions in four areas: setting or event strategies, antecedent strategies, behavior teaching strategies, and consequence strategies. The plan also contains details such as: who does what strategies when, where, how often and why; how emergency or crisis situations will be handled; and how implementation and effectiveness of the plan will be monitored (U.S. Department of Education, 2000). Browning-Wright (2003) views the positive behavior support plan as a proactive action plan that addresses behavior(s) impeding learning and delineates what positive behavioral interventions, strategies, and supports are needed, including: teaching an alternative or replacement behavior, making instructional and environmental changes, providing reinforcements, implementing reactive strategies, and maintaining effective communication based on the functional behavior assessment. The plan may include the following components (Van Haren & Fiedler, 2004, p. 19):

1. A summary of information from the functional behavior assessment
2. An objective and measurable description of the targeted serious behaviors and positive replacement behaviors
3. Goals and objectives specific to the targeted behavior
4. A detailed description of the behavioral interventions to be used and the circumstances for their use
5. Schedules for recording the frequency of interventions and demonstrations of replacement behaviors
6. Criteria for determining when the interventions will be phased out or replaced with less intensive or less frequent interventions
7. The extent to which interventions will be used in the students' homes and in other settings
8. Specific dates for the administrators or, in the case of a child with a disability, the IEP team to review the behavior intervention program's effectiveness

    Figure 4.5 will help you review the measurement of student behavior.

APPLICABLE INTERVENTIONS

A major component of the positive behavioral support process is to identify behavioral interventions, strategies, and supports to improve each student's learning and performance. When implementing interventions for a specific student, strategies usually encompass multiple perspectives. To help you to better understand how multiple

FIGURE 4.5

Take a Moment

Think About	Reflect	Respond
Measuring a student's behavior	Do you measure your students' behaviors?	
	How do you accomplish this?	

perspectives apply to individual behavior management, a specific example of a problem behavior is presented: The student does not remain on task. Additionally, strategies that are effective for students with oppositional and defiant classroom behaviors exemplify the use of multiple perspectives, and are included in this section to illustrate applicable strategies that may be used with your students, as appropriate.

ECOLOGICAL STRATEGIES FOR A STUDENT WHO DOES NOT REMAIN ON TASK

Ecological strategies are designed to increase the person/environment fit. The student is perceived as an integral part of the classroom. Interventions include developing skill, adjusting class expectations, or modifying the physical environment for a "better fit." Some examples of ecological intervention strategies for a student who does not remain on task are:

- Establish classroom rules to "work on task" and to "work quietly in seat."
- Set limits for completing assignments.
- Reduce auditory and visual stimuli for student.
- Present tasks in the most attractive and interesting manner.
- Position the student's work desk so that he or she is not visually distracted by others.
- Assist the student to complete class assignments.
- Reduce the number of assignments. Add new assignments when previous ones are completed.
- Be proactive. Design a schedule that will work for the student's success.
- Provide activities that increase the opportunity for "active participation."
- Make sure that the student has needed materials to perform the task and that those are the only materials in the desk.
- Assess the degree of task difficulty in relation to the student's ability to successfully perform the task.
- Be sure that the student understands the instructions/directions for the task. Present instructions in a variety of ways.
- Interact frequently with the student to maintain involvement in the activity.
- Develop an environment that is quiet and uncluttered (e.g., clean, well-lighted, fresh-smelling, and at a comfortable temperature).

BEHAVIORAL STRATEGIES FOR A STUDENT WHO DOES NOT REMAIN ON TASK

Behavioral interventions include measurement, evaluation, and behavior change techniques using modeling and reinforcement. Examples of behavioral intervention strategies for a student who has difficulty staying on task are:

- Choose a peer to model on-task behavior.
- Reinforce the student for attending to a task. Gradually increase the time required for reinforcement.

■ Provide an incentive along with a directive. "When you complete this assignment, you may use the computer."
■ Reward the student for staying on task for a certain amount of time.
■ Make participation in extracurricular activities dependent upon completion of task (be sure that the student is interested in the extracurricular activity!).
■ Write a contract with the student specifying what behavior is expected (establish a reasonable amount of time to stay on task) and what reinforcement will be given upon successful completion of the contract.
■ Reinforce those students in the classroom who demonstrate on-task behavior.

COGNITIVE STRATEGIES FOR A STUDENT WHO DOES NOT REMAIN ON TASK

Cognitive learning interventions increase the student's capacity for self-responsibility by developing social skills and problem-solving abilities through self-monitoring, instruction, and training. This intervention emphasizes the use of language, thoughts, and "verbal rehearsal" to change behavior. Examples of cognitive learning intervention strategies for a student who has difficulty staying on task are:

■ Encourage the student to develop a 30-second definition of his or her goal to help him or her stay on task and focused (e.g., I will write five spelling words without a reminder from the teacher to stay on task).
■ Encourage the student to manage his or her class performance by maintaining a chart of the amount of time spent on task.
■ Have the student ask himself or herself questions (e.g., "What's next?).
■ Have the student assemble all needed materials prior to beginning the task.

HUMANISTIC STRATEGIES FOR A STUDENT WHO DOES NOT REMAIN ON TASK

The teacher plays a major role within this intervention. The student is motivated to change behavior because the teacher is nonauthoritarian, empathetic, and nonjudgmental. In sum, the student wants to please the teacher because he or she likes the teacher. Intervention strategies based on this perspective for a student who has difficulty staying on task are:

■ Interact frequently with the student and assure the student that you are very aware and concerned of his or her difficulty staying on task.
■ Let the student know that his or her off-task behavior does not affect what you think about him or her. It doesn't make the student a "bad" person—it is just a behavior that needs to be understood, and make clear that you are there to help him or her to do that, not to punish the student.
■ Create a safe, respectful, and accepting learning environment for all students in your class. Let your students know that you accept them and you are there to teach them how to do the best in school.
■ Greet and compliment your student, when appropriate, and acknowledge him or her in as many positive ways as possible.
■ Read and learn about your student to assess why he or she does not remain on task. Is it a pattern of behavior? Is it related to home or family factors, medication reactions, fear, tension, stress, or perhaps biophysical reasons such as lack of sleep, food, or shelter? If you sincerely care about your student, your student will know and over time begin to trust you. The relationship that you establish with your student is the key to a successful humanistic perspective intervention strategy.

INTERVENTION STRATEGY DECISIONS

Many possible interventions can be implemented, and you may decide to use several strategies. Review the behavioral assessment data: go over notes and written behavior records; talk to other teachers, the psychologist, the student's parents, and, if available, your administrator, to see if patterns of behavior are present in multiple contexts, not just in your classroom. If needed or desired, get permission to asses your student on Durand's Motivational Assessment Scale (MAS). It is a simple and quick assessment that does not require verbal ability in order to assess motivational variables that sustain an identified targeted behavior. Information from this assessment can help you to determine a meaningful behavioral intervention for a specific student. You can find further information on this assessment in the Resource section at the end of this chapter.

INTERVENTIONS FOR STUDENTS WITH OPPOSITIONAL AND DEFIANT BEHAVIORS

Students with oppositional defiant classroom behaviors can be confrontational, vindictive, disruptive, and irritating, especially to teachers or other adults in positions of authority. Students with oppositional and defiant behaviors tend to resist control and manipulation from any adult (Salend & Sylvestre, 2005; Woolsey-Terrazas & Chavez, 2002). According to these authors, students with this disorder need structure: rules, laws, rewards, punishment, love, guidance, and, most important, a sense of safety. However, the more controlling an adult appears to be, the more oppositional the student becomes. Woolsey-Terrazas and Chavez (2002) propose the following strategies that have proven effective in the classroom when consistently implemented:

- Don't threaten your students. Threatening students with oppositional and defiant behavior allows them to test your ability to follow through.
- Clearly define the expected behaviors. Students with oppositional and defiant behavior search for the "gray areas" to justify their actions.
- Clearly define the consequences of compliant and noncompliant behavior. This provides a direct relationship between the behavior and the consequence and prevents getting into verbal confrontations.
- Always be firm and directive. This reduces students' challenges and justifications for their position.
- During confrontations, do not allow your emotions to rule; stay cool and calm. With students with oppositional and defiant behaviors, your anger demonstrates that they are in control (Woolsey-Terraza & Chavez, 2002, p. 12).

Figure 4.6 asks you to reflect on the available interventions you can use in your classroom.

FIGURE 4.6

Take a Moment

Think About	Reflect	Respond
The types of applicable interventions that you use in your classroom	Describe the behavioral interventions that you use. Do you think that they are effective? Why do you think that they are or are not effective?	

CONCLUSION

Theoretical perspectives influence the manner in which an individual approaches behavior management. Therefore, having an understanding of the major theoretical perspectives and their associated interventions is beneficial, particularly when working in the schools and with families. Although perspectives and approaches may vary, the federal special education regulations require that whenever a special education student exhibits behaviors that impede his or her learning or that of others, the IEP team must address the situation in the form of a positive behavior support plan. This chapter presents a description of the positive behavior support process by explaining a functional behavior assessment, federal components of a positive behavior support plan, and examples of interventions and strategies for improving student learning and performance.

EXPLORATIONS

1. List three intervention strategies that are used in the classroom. Next to each of these interventions, write the theoretical perspective that the intervention exemplifies. Provide a rationale as to why you selected the corresponding theoretical approach.
2. Have you ever participated in the development of a positive behavior support plan? If so, describe the benefits of this process. If not, why do you think this process would be beneficial to you as a classroom teacher?
3. What is the benefit of a functional behavior assessment (FBA)? Is there a student in your class or on your caseload that would benefit from having a functional behavior assessment conducted? How would you report these findings to the parent?
4. What are the federal legal components of a positive behavioral support plan?

WEBSITES

ADD—Attention Deficit Disorder
http://add.about.com/health/add/library/weekly/aa012598.htm
A resource site on ADD/ADHD.

Behavior Home Page, Kentucky
http://www.state.ky.us/agencies/behave/homepage.html
Addresses behavioral issues and provides intervention strategies, as well as links to professional organizations and federal laws concerning individuals with disabilities.

Center for Effective Collaboration and Practice
http://www.air.org/cecp
Describes services for students who have behavioral and emotional disorders.

Classroom Management
http://www.theteachersguide.com/ClassManagement.htm
This site has articles, Internet sites, discussion groups, printouts, and information on books about behavior management.

Classroom Management—School Environment (California Department of Education)
http://www.cde.ca.gov/ls/ss/se/classroommgmt.asp
This California Department of Education site provides a California Resource Guide for Classroom Management that contains chapters on preventing problem behavior, classroom organization and management, reinforcers, activities for creating a positive learning environment, teaching social skills, instructional strategies, communicating with parents/caregivers, behavioral assessment and related interventions, aggressive behaviors, and other problem behaviors.

Intervention Central Website

http://www.interventioncentral.org

Website for Intervention Central that offers free tools and resources to help school staff and parents promote positive classroom behaviors and foster effective learning. The site addresses content areas as well as behavioral supports.

Love and Logic

http://www.loveandlogic.com

This site describes the Love and Logic Process for teachers and parents, providing examples of enforceable statements, articles, resources, and contacts to learn more about this process.

PBIS Website

http://pbis.org

Presents information on the use of positive behavioral interventions and supports in multiple settings: home, school, and community. This site provides related research briefs, fact sheets, and case studies. The Technical Assistance Center on Positive Behavioral Interventions and Supports (PBIS) was established by the Office of Special Education Programs, U.S. Department of Education.

Positive Environments, Network of Trainers (PENT)

http://www.pent.ca.gov

This site provides guidelines for developing a positive support plan, recommendations for behavioral interventions, and links to other Websites on behavior management.

6 Seconds Website

http://www.6seconds.org

Provides resources on emotional intelligence and emotional quotient.

6 Seconds Website for Self-Science Curriculum

http://www.6seconds.org/school/self-science.php

Provides information on the *Self-Science* curriculum, a comprehensive approach to building emotional intelligence in schools.

REFERENCES

Browning Wright., D. (2003). Behavior/Discipline Trainings. Sacramento, CA.

Crone, D. A., & Horner, R. H. (2003). *Building positive behavior support systems in schools: Functional behavioral assessment.* New York: Gilford Press.

Dice, M. L. (1994). *Intervention strategies for children with emotional or behavioral disorders.* San Diego: Singular Publishing Group, Inc.

Hammill, D. D., & Bartel, N. R. (2004). *Teaching students with learning and behavior problems.* Austin, TX: PRO-ED.

Jones, V., & Jones, L. (2003). *Comprehensive classroom management: Creating communities of support and solving problems.* Boston: Pearson Education.

Lampi, A. R., Fenty, N. S., & Beaunae, C. (2005). Making the three Ps easier: Praise, proximity, and precorrection. *Beyond Behavior, 15*(1), 8–12.

Long, N. J., Wood, M. M., & Fecser, F. A. (2001). *Life space crisis intervention* (2nd ed.) Austin, TX: PRO-ED.

Maag, J. W. (1999). *Behavior management: From theoretical implications to practical applications.* San Diego: Singular Publishing.

Marzano, R. J., & Marzano, J. S. (2003). The key to classroom management. *Educational Leadership, 61*(1), 6–13.

McCarney, S. B. (2003). *Emotional or behavioral disorder intervention manual revised: Goals, objectives, and intervention strategies for the emotionally or behaviorally disordered student.* Columbia, MO: Hawthorne Educational Services.

Owens, L., & Dieker, L. A. (2003). How to spell success for secondary students labeled EBD: How students define effective teachers. *Beyond Behavior, 12*(2), 19–23.

Payne, L. D., Mancil, G. R., & Landers, E. (2005). Consequence-based behavioral interventions for classroom teachers. *Beyond Behavior, 15*(1), 13–20.

Peterson, R. L., Miller, C., & Skiba, R. J. (2004). A framework for planning safe and responsive schools. *Beyond Behavior, 13*(3), 12–16.

Rief, S. (2003). *The ADHA book of lists.* New York: National Professional Resources, Inc.

Rief, S. (2005). *How to reach and teach children with ADD/ADHD.* New York: National Professional Resources, Inc.

Salend, S. J., & Sylvestre, S. (2005). Understanding and addressing oppositional and defiant classroom behaviors. *Teaching Exceptional Children, 37*(6), 32–39.

Sugai, G., Horner, R. H., & Sprague, J. R. (1999). Functional-assessment-based behavior support planning: Research to practice to research. *Behavioral Disorders, 24*(3), 253–257.

United States Department of Education. (2000). 22nd Annual Report to Congress. Washington, D.C.

Van Haren, B. A., & Fiedler, C. (2004). Legal limits: Physical restraint and seclusion of students with disabilities. *Beyond Behavior, 13*(3), 17–19.

Walker, H. M., Ramsey, E., & Gresham, F. M. (2004). *Antisocial behavior in school: Evidence-based practices.* Canada: Thomson Wadsworth.

Williams, P. A., Alley, R. D., & Henson, K. T. (1999). *Managing secondary classrooms: Principles and strategies for effective management and instruction.* Needham Heights, MA: Allyn & Bacon.

Woolsey-Terrazas, W., & Chavez, J. A. (2002). Strategies to work with students with oppositional defiant disorder. *CEC Today, 8*(7), 12.

Wright, D. B., & Gurman, H. B. (2001). *Positive intervention for serious behavior problems: Best practices in implementing the Hughes Bill (Assembly Bill 2586) and the positive behavioral intervention regulations* (Rev. ed.) Sacramento: California Department of Education.

Ziff, B., & Zetlin, A. (2004). California State University, Los Angeles Education Specialist Intern Program Handbook. Los Angeles, CA.

RESOURCES

1. Motivation Assessment Scale by V. Mark Durand and Daniel Crimmins, published by Monaco and Associates.

   This very user-friendly assessment instrument has 16 Likert-scale items that the rater completes. The 16 items relate to a specific target behavior. Analysis of the responses indicates the type of motivation that is sustaining the behavior. Advantages of this assessment instrument are: (1) it is quick and relatively inexpensive to administer; (2) students with moderate to severe learning needs benefit because verbal ability is not needed to complete this assessment, and the cognitive functioning level may vary.

2. Courage to Change: Catalog for Life's Challenges, toll-free number is 1-800-440-4003.

   This mail-order catalog includes professional resources and instructional self-help games, activities, and books for a wide range of ages and topics.

3. *Imagination: Activities that Allow Students to Get Up on Their Feet and Move* by Bobbi Kidder published by Cottonwood Press, Inc. 2nd edition 2001.

    This publication includes 33 activities that can be used in the classroom setting to increase students' communication skills, confidence, and risk taking abilities. Students participate in active learning that results in the ability to work more effectively in a team-oriented environment.

5

Assessment for Instruction

"I have not failed. I've just found 10,000 ways that won't work."
Thomas Alva Edison (1847–1931)

CHAPTER OBJECTIVES

- Discuss the response to intervention model
- Describe the purpose of linking assessment to teaching
- Present informal measures of assessment

> *Before reading this chapter, think about how you view assessment and teaching. What value do you see assessment having in your classroom? What assessments are you using and why are you choosing them? In what ways might assessments inform teaching? Record your reflections and revisit your response as you read this chapter.*

INTRODUCTION

Assessment is a critical part of the teaching process. This chapter addresses the value of assessment in instructional planning and ways of collecting information to make informed decisions to establish an appropriate learning environment based on students' strengths and weaknesses. According to Bransford, Brown, and Cocking (2000), aligning assessment with principles of learning involves teachers taking the responsibility for providing a sound instructional program by mirroring instruction with the assessment and identifying the many opportunities that exist within the instructional program to assess ongoing student progress. The matrix in Figure 5.1 provides an overview of the assessment decisions.

It is important that you understand the terms associated with assessment (Figure 5.2), and are able to discuss these terms with your students' parents/guardians. To assist you a glossary of terms is included in the Resources section of this chapter. You will be conducting formal and informal assessments as a special educator. You need to learn the purposes of different types of measurements, the vocabulary associated with assessment, and how to incorporate assessment into your educational planning. You need to understand all the assessments that your special education students experience. This chapter provides a quick reference to information on assessment.

FIGURE 5.1

Summary
Assessment
Decisions

Source: Salvia, John and
James E. Ysseldyke,
Assessment in Special and
Remedial Education,
Eighth Edition. Copyright
© 2001 by Houghton
Mifflin Company. Adapted
with permission.

- Prereferral classroom decisions
- Screening, eligibility decisions
- Instructional planning decisions
- Program decisions

Term	Definition
Assessment	Refers to your gathering of quantitative and qualitative of information about your students.
Test	Refers to the specific type of assessment you use to determine your students' learning levels.
Measurement	Refers to the quantitative description of the results of the tests.
Norm-referenced	Standardized, formal procedures for administering, timing, and scoring. They have been "normed" or administered to a representative sample of similar age or grade-level students so that final test results can be compared to students of similar characteristics. Test results indicate a person's relative performance in the group. These standardized tests must be administered as specified in the manual to ensure valid and reliable results.
Criterion-referenced	Measure what the person is able to do and indicate what skills have been mastered. A criterion-referenced test (CRT) compares a person's performance with his or her own past performance. The emphasis is on assessing specific and relevant behaviors that have been mastered rather than indicating the relative standing in the group.

FIGURE 5.2

Key Assessment Terms

RESPONSE TO INTERVENTION MODEL

Some school districts use the response to intervention (RTI) model to identify students with learning disabilities for special education services. This model is based on the documentation by general education teachers of effective instructional practices with the achievement level of students, matching assessment results with research-based instruction, along with continued monitoring during intervention efforts. With this model, students receive assistance when needed, as opposed to waiting for them to fail and being recommended to special education. The RTI model requires some type of initial screening, followed by high-quality instruction (Tier I), monitoring of the student's response to the intervention efforts (Tier II), and if the student does not respond to intense intervention efforts, a special education referral to determine whether or not the student meets the requirements for special education services is the next step (Tier III).

Allington (2006) cautions teachers on the negative impact of fragmenting instruction based on the three-tier model. Students do not benefit from a Title 1 teacher using one reading program and the classroom teacher using another. If the assessment shows a student is weak in comprehension strategies, then good practice dictates that teachers work together on that weakness using the curriculum, not by introducing commercial reading packages. Special education teachers who participate in grade-level meetings with general education teachers need to discuss the importance of analyzing each student's data results to determine the specific type of instruction needed and how all the student's teachers can work together to implement the plan.

This prereferral strategy provides evidence that students receive good instruction and necessary corrective interventions, but students' lack of success as documented through multiple assessments shows the need for special education services. Special education teachers can use this prereferral assessment data in planning effective instruction.

LINKING ASSESSMENT TO TEACHING

Assessment is a continuous process that allows teachers to make informed decisions about teaching effectiveness and students' achievement. Teachers are not able document students' annual growth and make appropriate instructional decisions without knowing how students are progressing in the standards, which are typically measured with school district standardized tests (McLoughlin & Lewis, 2005).

For many students receiving special education services, standardized tests scores may not be representative of how successfully each student has met the standards, but the scores do provide one measure for teachers to use in evaluation and planning. To learn more about the formal assessments used in the school, teachers might:

- Ask to see the samples and speak with other special educators about preparing students for these tests.
- Note whether the tests are norm-referenced or criterion-referenced measures.
- Discuss with colleagues how students with exceptionalities typically perform and how the results are used in the school.

To gain specific performance information, teachers need to study each student's record for assessment data, lists of strengths and weaknesses, recommendations for a testing environment, and testing modifications. Salend (2005) recommends that as the IEP team considers any testing accommodations, they develop a rating scale showing how successful a past accommodation was in helping the student demonstrate learning to determine future testing environments.

Being an effective teacher requires deciding what to teach and how to teach it, as well as how to present the information, monitor the learning, and analyze student data to improve the instructional environment. Creating an effective learning environment is based on classroom evaluations that provide current information on students' abilities. Analyzing students' data guides teachers in connecting appropriate expectations with lesson objectives (Alexandrin, 2003). This point supports the need to consider each student's needs as documented on some type of assessment, plan for the outcomes, and strategize for implementing instruction. In developing lessons:

- Review the appropriate standards and IEPs.
- Determine what the outcomes need to be for each student.
- Think about how to engage each student to achieve the outcomes. The teaching focus is on the expected outcomes, which are not necessarily the same for all students.
- Plan the strategy to include the behavioral objectives for the students, the activities for the students to practice their learning, and a variety of assessments to measure achievement. Instructional planning involves decision making based on specific areas of need as documented through assessments. Figure 5.3 asks you to reflect on your assessment experiences as a student.

FIGURE 5.3
FIGURE 5.3
Take a Moment

Think About	Reflect	Respond
Experiences with assessment as a student	What kinds of tests do you remember from your elementary and secondary levels that you felt adequately represented your achievement?	

INFORMAL METHODS OF ASSESSMENT

Assessment is ongoing: formative and diagnostic. These measures provide data to make informed decisions about developing an effective teaching strategy. According to Ward (2005), teachers need to assess students using curriculum standards before they plan an intervention for students with exceptionalities. Following this process allows students to acquire the skills and strategies needed to be successful. Equally important is for students to understand how they are being evaluated for each assignment, and what the rubric guidelines are to indicate successful performance (Kerrins & Cushing, 1996).

SYSTEMATIC OBSERVATION

Teachers informally observe students daily. By recording students' responses and analyzing their errors, teachers are able to make informed instructional changes. This is assessment linked to instruction. For example, you might use task and error analysis as some students work at the board, on the computer, or in small groups to evaluate their learning and make diagnostic instructional decisions.

Consider the following suggestions:

- After thinking about the types of errors students may be making, plan the intervention strategy to target the specific areas of concern.
- After reteaching, observe students again to analyze the success of the intervention.
- Use a rubric to keep track of the students' progress.
- Add notes to support evaluation. These notes might mention whether students worked alone or in small groups, or needed prompting to achieve an acceptable level.

At this point teachers decide whether or not additional interventions are needed immediately. Many times the skill/strategy will be reinforced through successive lessons. Figure 5.4 shows sample observation notes.

CHECKLISTS

You may use a commercial checklist or one you create to document mastery of specific skills. Roach and Elliott (2005) suggest applying a numerical rubric to your observations to document students' performance. You might use the results to group students for additional direct instruction, for independent practice work, or for placement decisions. Stanford and Reeves (2005) suggest using a checklist that has been shared with the students prior to its use to informally document degrees of performance. For example, using specific terms such as *always*, *sometimes*, *with assistance*, or *never* may provide more accurate information than simply a yes or no. Maroney, Finson, Beaver, and Jensen (2003) suggest recording the importance of each skill beside the level of achievement on the checklist to assist you in making diagnostic decisions. Is the skill important to learning at the next level, such as developing letter/sound awareness before phoneme substitution? Figure 5.5 provides a sample checklist.

Consider your district standards, your students' exceptionalities, and the content you are teaching as you develop a checklist to document your students' success with the material. Use this information to provide diagnostic teaching when necessary.

Think about the sample checklist in Figure 5.6 and consider how you would use this information to plan instruction.

- How can you support this student in developing interpretive skills when reading?
- What assistance might you offer to guide the student in understanding new vocabulary by using content information?

Checklists can also be used to document your students' progress. Figure 5.5 is an example of how a teacher can use a checklist to document progress for a kindergarten student and Figure 5.6 is a sample checklist for a fifth-grade student in an English class.

CURRICULUM-BASED EVALUATIONS

Curriculum-based assessment (CBA) and curriculum-based measurement (CBM) are two types of structured evaluations that use selected items from grade-level curriculum. These evaluations, which can be commercially produced or teacher-made, provide detailed data to inform instructional planning. CBM scores provide data based on timed responses, while CBA scores may or may not reflect timed responses. Use of both these forms of assessment

FIGURE 5.4
Sample Observation Notes

Student	Observed Math Work	Analysis
R.W.	$2 \times 4 = 6$	Adds, doesn't multiply
D.T.	$1/2 + 2/5 = 3/7$	Adds numerators and denominators; doesn't convert fractions
A.S.	$x = 2$; $12x/3x = 4x$	Divides numbers correctly but doesn't use x equivalent to solve problem

FIGURE 5.5
Sample Checklist
Kelly T. (Kindergarten)

Skill	Importance	Score 1–5 (5 meaning mastery)
Recognizes the letters of the alphabet	Extremely necessary	5 (points to and names letter)
Retells a story	Necessary	3 (needs prompting to tell what happened at the beginning, middle, and end)
Rhymes words	Necessary	2 (able to rhyme "t", "ly" but does not seem to hear "p" correctly)

FIGURE 5.6
Sample Checklist
George S.—English
(Fifth grade)

Skill	Importance	Score 1–5 (5 meaning mastery)
Response to fact questions	Extremely	5
Response to interpretive questions	Very	2 (no evidence of being able to read on own and put information together)
Use context to understanding new vocabulary	Somewhat	3 (understands more if the terms are explained prior to the reading)

will provide the teacher with diagnostic information on students' success on timed and not-timed tests.

TEACHER-MADE TESTS

In preparing your tests, think about two modalities: how you will present it and how the students will respond (Ysseldyke, 2004). Teachers may even ask students to reflect on how they want to be assessed, once the content objectives and expected outcomes are understood. Teachers rarely rely on one assessment to judge the effectiveness of the lesson, so there are opportunities throughout the lesson for students to demonstrate progress through many modalities.

- For some students you may provide a fill-in-the-blank paper, a multiple-choice test, true/false statements, open-ended inquiries, or oral questioning.
- For other students you may provide a summary paper with key terms missing so that they can supply the appropriate concepts.

Consider the IEP test adaptation and modification requirements for each of your students in developing their tests (reading, writing, math, extended-time issues).

- What is the best modality for each of your students to demonstrate their learning? Besides written responses, think about PowerPoint presentations, projects, or oral responses to test items being read aloud.
- Talk to your students about the objectives and the expected outcomes for your lessons.
- Ask them to reflect on the best way to represent their learning.
- Provide them with the rubric prior to their beginning the assessment to help them understand the expectations (Kerrins and Cushing, 1996).

ASSESSMENT PORTFOLIOS

There are many types of portfolios, such as those that are representative of each student's accomplishments and those that are showcases. Another type is the assessment portfolio, which can provide evaluations aligned with a student's IEP to reflect the purpose for which it exists. Teachers and students may work together to decide the work to include in the portfolio that will demonstrates a range of skills and knowledge. Figure 5.7 asks you to reflect on your assessment practices as a special educator.

FIGURE 5.7

Think About	Reflect	Respond
Experiences with assessment as a special education teacher	What types of assessments have you used or observed in the classroom setting? Do the assessments used accurately reflect what the students know? If not, why not? Have you ever made adjustments to your instructional approach based on your students' current progress? If so, explain.	

CONCLUSION

As you analyze your students' needs based on your assessment measures, remember that assessment is ongoing: formative and diagnostic. These measures provide you with the data to make informed decisions about your teaching, which includes your method of presentation, guided practice to support students' learning, and materials for independent practice to assess learning. Although you may be using your grade-level standards, your responsibility lies in determining how to present the information to allow for your students to be successful.

Effective teachers use formal and informal assessment data to plan daily instruction. This requires the teacher to analyze students' yearly growth against grade-level standards, develop annual goals for students' IEPs, create lessons that meet students' needs, and monitor students' achievement levels. Informal measures allow the teacher to track each student's progress and plan accordingly.

EXPLORATIONS

1. Think about the formal and informal assessment results for one student in your class. Prepare an outline summarizing these results and address how you would develop a more effective instructional program for this student.
2. What types of assessment do you feel are more valuable to help you diagnose your students' strengths and weaknesses? Create a table outlining the tests you use and the information you gain from them.
3. Present one case study to your colleagues that focuses on your assessment process and how you link assessment to instruction.
4. Make a list of the assessments available to you as the special education teacher. Include in this list the value of each of these assessments in planning your instruction.
5. Create an overview of the response to intervention model to share with colleagues in order to promote discussions regarding assessment and instruction.

WEBSITES

Center for Innovations in Education

http://www.cise.missouri.edu/publications/innovations/november-2005/beldin.html

This site provides basic information on RTI with links to sites about co-teaching and differentiated instruction.

Educational Technology Clearinghouse

http://etc.usf.edu/assessmt/

This site provides links for assessment, technology, and teaching ideas.

EDUTOPIA, The New World of Learning

http://www.edutopia.org/assessment

This site suggests using performance assessment to gauge student learning.

Family Education

http://school.familyeducation.com/educational-testing/educational-philosophy/38778.html

This site includes an article by J. Popham on the problems with standardized achievement tests.

International Reading Association

http://www.reading.org/resources/issues/focus_nclb_IDEA_RTI.html

This site provides information about RTI, its effect on minority students, and the roles of teachers.

Kathy Schrock's Guide for Educators

http://school.discovery.com/schrockguide/assess.html

This site provides information on assessments and rubrics.

Learning Disabilities Organization

http://www.ld.org/Advocacy/kids_learning.cfm

This site provides information on identifying students before they fail.

LD Online

http://www.ldonline.org/ld_indepth/assessment/response_to_intervention.html

This site offers basic information on the RTI model and provides more information about the discrepancy model that RTI replaces.

National Association of State Directors of Special Education

http://www.nasdse.org

This site provides information on implementing the response to intervention model.

National Center for Progress Monitoring

http://www.studentprogress.org

This site provides technical assistance and professional development to states about the use of ongoing curriculum-based assessment to monitor students' academic growth.

NEA Professional Library

http://www.nea.org/teachexperience/ask030508.html

This site provides ideas on documenting students' knowledge and skills.

North Central Regional Educational Laboratory (NCREL)

http://www.ncrel.org/policy/pubs/html/beyond/stakes.htm

This site provides information on learning how to use data.

PBS Teacher Source

http://www.pbs.org/teachersource/whats_new/math/assessment0500.shtm

This site suggests using interviews as an assessment tool.

Reading Rockets

http://www.readingrockets.org/article/173

This site provides a parent's guide to standardized testing.

RTI_Wire

http://www.jimwrightonline.com/php/rti/rti_wire.php

This site provides a directory of RTI resources.

Texas Reading Center

http://www.texasreading.org/3tier

This site provides information about the three-tier reading model in K–3 classes and appropriate placement in special education based on needs.

University of Southern California, Center for Excellence in Teaching

http://www.aare.edu.au/02pap/iza02378.htm

This site discusses the purposes and problems of assessment.

WestEd

http://www.wested.org/cs/we/view/feat/48

This site provides information for an alternative way to identify students with learning disabilities.

Wrightslaw: From Emotion to Advocacy

http://www.fetaweb.com/06/glossary.assessment.htm

This site provides a glossary of assessment terms.

REFERENCES

Alexandrin, J. (2003). Using continuous, constructive classroom evaluations. *Teaching Exceptional Children, 36*(1), 52–57.

Allington, R. (2006). Research and the three tier model. *Reading Today, 32*(4), 20.

Bransford, J., Brown, A., & Cocking, R. (2000). *How people learn: Brain, mind, experience, and school*. Washington, DC: National Academy Press.

Horowitz, S. (2006). Response to intervention: A primer. Retrieved April 2, 2006 from *http://www.ncld.org/index.php?option=content&task=view&aid=498.*

Kerrins, J., & Cushing, K. (1996). Gotcha or rubrics? Instruction and assessment of graduate students. *Journal of Excellence in College Teaching, 7*(3), 31–56.

Kovaleski, J., & Prasse, D. (2004). Response to instruction in the identification of learning disabilities: A guide for school teams. Retrieved April 2, 2006 from *http://www.nasponline.org/publications/cq324instruction.html.*

Maroney, S., Finson, K., Beaver, J., & Jensen, M. (2003). Preparing for successful inquiry in inclusive science classrooms. *Teaching Exceptional Children, 3*(1), 18–25.

McLoughlin, J., & Lewis, R. (2005). *Assessing students with special needs* (6th ed.). Upper Saddle River, NJ: Merrill/Prentice Hall.

Orlich, D., Harder, R., Callahan, R., & Gibson, H. (2001). *Teaching strategies: A guide to better instruction*. New York: Houghton Mifflin.

Roach, A., & Elliott, S. (2005). Goal attainment scaling: An efficient and effective approach to monitoring student progress. *Teaching Exceptional Children, 37*(4), 8–17.

Salend, S. (2005). Report card models that support communication and differentiation of instruction. *Teaching Exceptional Children, 37*(4), 28–34.

Stanford, P., & Reeves, S. (2005). Assessment that drives instruction. *Teaching Exceptional Children, 37*(4), 18–22.

Ward, H. (2005). The use of language experiences in teaching reading to students with severe learning disabilities. *The Reading Matrix, 5*(1), 16–20.

Wright, A. (2001). The ABCs of assessment: Aligning assessment with instruction. Retrieved April 2006 from *http://www.nsta.org/main/news/pdf/tst0110_60.pdf.*

Ysseldyke, S. (2004). *Assessment in special and inclusive education*. Boston, MA: Houghton Mifflin.

RESOURCES

GLOSSARY OF TERMS ASSOCIATED WITH TESTING

Glossary is reproduced from *What Does Research Say About Assessment?* by R.J. Dietel, J.L. Herman, and R.A. Knuth. Copyright © 1991 North Central Regional Educational Laboratory at Learning Point Associates. Used with permission of Learning Point Associates.

Achievement test An examination that measures educationally relevant skills or knowledge about such subjects as reading, spelling, or mathematics.

Age norms Values representing typical or average performance of people of certain age groups.

Authentic task A task performed by students that has a high degree of similarity to tasks performed in the real world.

Average A statistic that indicates the central tendency or most typical score of a group of scores. Most often "average" refers to the sum of a set of scores divided by the number of scores in the set.

Battery A group of carefully selected tests that are administered to a given population, the results of which are of value individually, in combination, and totally.

Ceiling The upper limit of ability that can be measured by a particular test.

Criterion-referenced test A measurement of achievement of specific criteria or skills in terms of absolute levels of mastery. The focus is on performance of an individual as measured against a standard or criteria rather than against performance of others who take the same test, as with norm-referenced tests.

Diagnostic test An intensive, in-depth evaluation process with a relatively detailed and narrow coverage of a specific area. The purpose of this test is to determine the specific learning needs of individual students and to be able to meet those needs through regular or remedial classroom instruction.

Dimensions, traits, or subscales The subcategories used in evaluating a performance or portfolio product (e.g., in evaluating student writing one might rate student performance on subscales such as organization, quality of content, mechanics, style).

Domain-referenced test A test in which performance is measured against a well-defined set of tasks or body of knowledge (domain). Domain-referenced tests are a specific set of criterion-referenced tests and have a similar purpose.

Grade equivalent The estimated grade level that corresponds to a given score.

Holistic scoring Scoring based upon an overall impression (as opposed to traditional test scoring, which counts up specific errors and subtracts points on the basis of them). In holistic scoring the rater matches his or her overall impression to the point scale to see how the portfolio product or performance should be scored. Raters usually are directed to pay attention to particular aspects of a performance in assigning the overall score.

Informal test A nonstandardized test that is designed to give an approximate index of an individual's level of ability or learning style; often teacher-constructed.

Inventory A catalog or list for assessing the absence or presence of certain attitudes, interests, behaviors, or other items regarded as relevant to a given purpose.

Item An individual question or exercise in a test or evaluative instrument.

Norm Performance standard that is established by a reference group and that describes average or typical performance. Usually norms are determined by testing a representative group and then calculating the group's test performance.

Norm-referenced test An objective test that is standardized on a group of individuals whose performance is evaluated in relation to the performance of others; contrasted with criterion-referenced test.

Normal curve equivalent Standard scores with a mean of 40 and a standard deviation of approximately 21.

Objective percent correct The percent of the items measuring a single objective that a student answers correctly.

Percent score The percent of items that are answered correctly.

Percentile The percent of people in the norming sample whose scores were below a given score.

Performance assessment An evaluation in which students are asked to engage in a complex task, often involving the creation of a product. Student performance is rated based on the process the student engages in and/or based on the product of his or her task. Many performance assessments emulate actual workplace activities or real-life skill applications that require higher-order processing skills. Performance assessments can be individual or group-oriented.

Performance criteria A predetermined list of observable standards used to rate performance assessments. Effective performance criteria include considerations for validity and reliability.

Performance standards The levels of achievement pupils must reach to receive particular grades in a criterion-referenced grading system (e.g., higher than 90 receives an A, between 80 and 89 receives a B, etc.) or to be certified at particular levels of proficiency.

Portfolio A collection of representative student work over a period of time. A portfolio often documents a student's best work, and may include a variety of other kinds of process information (e.g., drafts of student work, students' self-assessment of their work, parents' assessments). Portfolios may be used for evaluation of a student's abilities and improvement.

Process The intermediate steps a student takes in reaching the final performance or end product specified by the prompt. Process includes all strategies, decisions, rough drafts, and rehearsals—whether deliberate or not—used in completing the given task.

Prompt An assignment or directions asking the student to undertake a task or series of tasks. A prompt presents the context of the situation, the problem or problems to be solved, and criteria or standards by which students will be evaluated.

Published test A test that is publicly available because it has been copyrighted and published commercially.

Rating scales A written list of performance criteria associated with a particular activity or product that an observer or rater uses to assess the pupil's performance on each criterion in terms of its quality.

Raw score The number of items that are answered correctly.

Reliability The extent to which a test is dependable and consistent when administered to the same individuals on different occasions. Technically, this is a statistical term that defines the extent to which errors of measurement are absent from a measurement instrument.

Rubric A set of guidelines for giving scores. A typical rubric states all the dimensions being assessed, contains a scale, and helps the rater place the given work properly on the scale.

Screening A fast, efficient measurement for a large population to identify individuals who may deviate in a specified area, such as the incidence of maladjustment or readiness for academic work.

Specimen set A sample set of testing materials that is available from a commercial test publisher. The sample may include a complete individual test without multiple copies or a copy of the basic test and administration procedures.

Standard scores A score that is expressed as a deviation from a population mean.

Standardized test A form of measurement that has been normed against a specific population. Standardization is obtained by administering the test to a given population and then calculating means, standard deviations, standardized scores, and percentiles. Equivalent scores are then produced for comparisons of an individual score to the norm group's performance.

Stanine One of the steps in a nine-point scale of standard scores.

Task A goal-directed assessment activity demanding that students use their background of knowledge and skill in a continuous way to solve a complex problem or question.

Validity The extent to which a test measures what it was intended to measure. Validity indicates the degree of accuracy of either predictions or inferences based upon a test score.

RESOURCES

TYPES OF UNSTRUCTURED ASSESSMENT TECHNIQUES

Adapted from the National Clearinghouse for Bilingual Education (*http://www.ncela.gwu.edu/pubs/pigs/pig3.htm*).

Anecdotal This method can be used by teachers to record behaviors and students' progress. These comments can include behavioral, emotional, and academic information. For instance, "Jaime sat for 5 minutes before beginning his assignment." These should be written carefully, avoiding judgmental words.

Brainstorming This technique can be used successfully with all ages of children to determine what may already be known about a particular topic. Students often feel free to participate because there is no criticism or judgment.

Debates Students' oral work can be evaluated informally in debates by assessing their oral presentation skills in terms of their ability to understand concepts and present them to others in an orderly fashion.

Games Games can provide students with a challenging method for increasing their skills in various areas such as math, spelling, naming categories of objects/people, and so on.

Homework Any written work students do alone, either in class or in the home, can be gathered and used to assess student progress. With teacher guidance, students can participate in diagnosing and remediating their own errors. In addition, students' interests, abilities, and efforts can be monitored across time.

Logs or journals An individual method of writing. Teachers can review on a daily, weekly, or quarterly basis to determine how students perceive their learning processes as well as to shape their ideas and strengths for more formal writing that occurs in other activities.

Naturalistic Related to anecdotal records, this type of observation may take the form of notes written at the end of the day by a teacher. They may record what occurred on the playground, in the classroom, among students, or they may just reflect the general classroom atmosphere.

Story retelling This technique can be used in either oral or written formats. It provides information on a wide range of language-based abilities. Recall is part of retelling, but teachers can use it to determine whether children understood the point of the story and what problems children have in organizing the elements of the story into a coherent whole. This also can be used to share cultural heritage when children are asked to retell a story in class that is part of their family heritage.

Writing samples When students write anything on specific topics, their products can be scored by using one of the available techniques. Other creative writing samples that can be used to assess student progress include newspapers, newsletters, collages, graffiti walls, scripts for a play, and language experience stories.

TYPES OF STRUCTURED INFORMAL ASSESSMENTS

Checklists Checklists specify student behaviors or products expected during progression through the curriculum. The items on the checklist may be content-area objectives. A checklist is considered to be a type of observational technique. Because observers check only the presence or absence of the behavior or product, checklists generally are reliable and relatively easy to use. Used over time, checklists can document students' rate and degree of accomplishment within the curriculum.

Cloze tests Cloze tests are composed of text from which words have been deleted randomly. Students fill in the blanks based on their comprehension of the context of the passage. The procedure is intended to provide a measure of reading comprehension.

Criterion-referenced tests Criterion-referenced tests are sometimes included as a type of informal assessment. This type of test is tied directly to instructional objectives, measures progress through the curriculum, and can be used for specific instructional planning. In order for the test to reflect a particular curriculum, criterion-referenced tests often are developed locally by teachers or a school district. Student performance is evaluated relative to mastery of the objectives, with a minimum performance level being used to define mastery.

Miscue analysis An informal assessment of strategies used by students when reading aloud or retelling a story. Typically, students read a grade-level passage (e.g., 240 words) while a judge follows along with a duplicate copy of the passage. The student may be tape-recorded. Each time an error occurs, the judge circles the word or phrase. A description of the actual error can be taken from the tape after the session and analyzed for errors in pronunciation, sentence structure, vocabulary, use of syntax, etc.

Questionnaires A questionnaire is a self-report assessment device on which students can provide information about areas of interest to the teacher. Questionnaire items can be written in a variety of formats and may be forced-choice (response alternatives are provided) or open-ended (students answer questions in their own words). Questionnaires designed to provide alternative assessments of achievement or language proficiency may ask students to report how well they believe they are performing in a particular subject or to indicate areas in which they would like more help from the teacher. One type of questionnaire (which assumes that the student can read in the native language) requests that students check off in the first language the kinds of things they can do in English. For a questionnaire to provide accurate information, students must be able to read the items, have the information to respond to the items, and have the writing skills to respond.

Rating scales This is an assessment technique often associated with observation of student work or behaviors. Rather than recording the presence or absence of a behavior or skill, the observer subjectively rates each item according to some dimension of interest. For example, students might be rated on how proficient they are on different elements of an oral presentation to the class. Each element may be rated on a 1 to 4 scale, with 4 representing the highest level of proficiency.

Structured interviews Structured interviews are essentially oral interview questionnaires. Used as an alternative assessment of achievement or language proficiency, the interview could be conducted with a student or a group of students to obtain information of interest to a teacher. As with written questionnaires, interview questions could be forced-choice or open-ended. Because the information exchange is entirely oral, it is important to keep interview questions (including response alternatives for forced-choice items) as simple and to the point as possible.

RESOURCES

SAMPLE DESCRIPTIONS OF STANDARDIZED ASSESSMENTS

Clinical Evaluation of Language Fundamental—Preschool: Charles E. Merrill Publishing Company.

> The assessment identifies nature and degree of language disabilities in the language areas of processing, production, and speech sounds.

McCarthy Scales of Children's Abilities: The Psychological Corporation.

> The McCarthy tests children ages 2 1/2 to 8 1/2. The purpose of the test is to evaluate the general intelligence level of children. It also identifies strengths and weaknesses in several ability areas. These areas include: verbal, perceptual-performance, quantitative, memory, motor, and general cognitive skills.

Peabody Picture Vocabulary Test (PPVT-R): American Guidance Service.

> The Peabody tests ages 2 1/2 to age 40. The purpose of the test is to measure vocabulary in English and nonverbal receptive (hearing) vocabulary. The test uses picture recognition for single word vocabulary.

Preschool Language Scale—3 (PLS-3): The Psychological Corporation.

> This test is designed for children ages birth through 6. The test assesses areas of language including auditory comprehension and expressive communication.

Sequenced Inventory for Communication Development—Revised (SICD): Slosson Educational Publications.

> The SICD assesses children ages 4 months to 4 years. The test assesses areas of expressive and receptive language skills.

Stanford-Binet Intelligence Scale—Fourth Edition: The Riverside Publishing Company.

The Stanford-Binet tests individuals who are ages 2 to 23. The test measures general intelligence. It focuses on the areas of verbal reasoning, quantitative reasoning, abstract/visual reasoning, and short-term memory.

Test of Early Language Development (TELD). Pro.ed Publisher.

The TELD assesses children ages 3 through 7 on language development.

Transdisciplinary Play-Based Assessment (TBA): Paul H. Brookes Publishing Company.

This informal assessment is for children birth through age 6. Through play children can be assessed in areas of cognition, social-emotional, communication and language, and sensorimotor skills.

Vineland Adaptive Behavior Scale (VABS). Pearson Assessments. The Vineland tests infants to children ages 18 and 11 months.

The purpose of the test is to assess social competence. The areas of assessment include communication, daily living, socialization, and motor skills.

Wechsler Preschool and Primary Scale of Intelligence—Revised (WPPSI-R): The Psychological Corporation.

A standardized test for children ages 4 1/2 to 6. It assesses areas of language and perception.

6

Instructional Planning

"Education is not the filling of a pail, but the lighting of a fire."

William Butler Yeats

CHAPTER OBJECTIVES

- Discuss instructional planning considerations
- Describe planning for assessment alternatives
- Present universal design for learning
- Review academic learning time

> *Before you read this chapter, think about the factors you take into consideration as you plan your lessons. What is the starting point for your planning? Have you analyzed why some lessons seem to be more effective than others? Record your reflections and revisit your response as you read this chapter.*

INTRODUCTION

This chapter discusses how to establish an instructional program based on the needs of students. When teachers know and understand the exceptionalities of each student, they are ready to plan instruction. Marzano (2003) suggests it is the combination of teaching experience, background knowledge, classroom curriculum design, and instructional strategies that contributes to a teacher becoming effective in establishing the environment for all students to achieve their goals.

Powell and Napoliello (2005) identify several principles to consider in planning differentiated instruction: knowledge of the student, the content, a variety of teaching strategies, and the ability to collaboratively plan instruction based on assessment and reflection. In planning a lesson, a teacher needs to consider specific objectives of the lesson, the structure for presenting the information in an organized manner, the specific activities to engage the students in their learning, and the types of assessment to document students' achievement. Based on this planning, the teacher manages, delivers, and evaluates the instruction (Ysseldyke, 2004). In making instructional decisions, teachers consider:

- Reviewing previously learned materials essential to understanding new material
- Collecting a variety of materials to support all students in their learning
- Selecting an appropriate strategy for the content
- Planning for motivation and mnemonic needs
- Planning assessment alternatives
- Incorporating assistive technology
- Monitoring academic learning time

In reading this chapter teachers are reminded that those who are organized and systematic in their planning are better able to deliver lessons more effectively (Orlich, Harder, Callahan, & Gibson, 2001). Figure 6.1 presents an instructional decision-making model.

INSTRUCTIONAL PLANNING CONSIDERATIONS

Effective teachers know more than the curriculum and the standards. They know their students and make good instructional decisions based on what affects student achievement. Because teachers work with students who are experiencing a variety of exceptionalities, several factors have to be considered in planning lessons to promote student success. As teachers gain experience, they are able to develop effective lesson plans based on all the factors significant to students' progress, rather than adapting lessons after considering each student's needs.

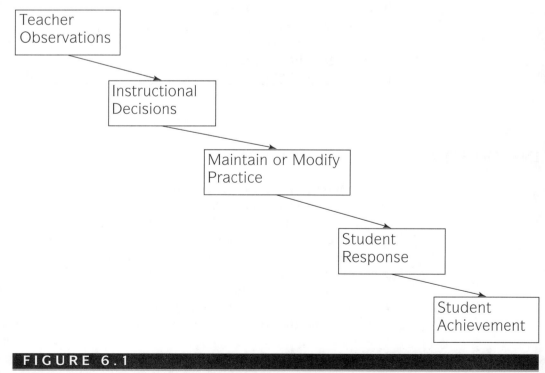

FIGURE 6.1

Instructional Decision-Making Model

Source: Assessment of At-Risk and Special Needs Children (p. 6), by J. Witt, S. Elliott, E. Daly, F. Gresham, & Kramer, 1998, Boston, MA: McGraw Hill. Reproduced with permission of the McGraw-Hill Companies.

NEEDS OF STUDENTS

Students' records provide the latest test scores, their strengths and weaknesses, and their annual measurable objectives. These records may document the effects of quality instructional interventions used prior to identifying any of the students with special needs. This information provides useful background information in planning instruction.

In addition to studying the records to gain information about each student, teachers also consider the following ideas prior to developing an instructional program:

■ Speaking with students' parents/guardians/teachers
■ Analyzing students' work samples for strengths and needs
■ Conducting informal assessments to provide current information to supplement information in the records
■ Studying the state standards for the grade levels and considering how to structure the program based on the students' performance levels
■ Analyzing the texts and materials to be used
■ Speaking with more experienced teachers who can provide insights on connecting students' needs, grade-level objectives, materials, and standards

With this information teachers develop ideas on matching instructional interventions with students' current performance levels and abilities. Figure 6.2 presents examples of instructional responses to student information.

BACKGROUND KNOWLEDGE

When introducing a literature piece, a chapter in a social studies/science book, or a math concept, the teacher needs to have an organization structure to present the material and guide students in their understanding and success with the content. Teachers first determine what students already know about the subject. They can do this through some type of visual graphic, such as a KWL chart as shown in Figure 6.3.

FIGURE 6.2
Sample Responses to Student Information

- Performance levels below grade level
- Skill levels not matched to grade-level materials
- Needs teacher supervision to achieve
- Poor performance on standardized tests
- Acceptable performance on informal measures

FIGURE 6.3
KWL Chart Example: Shock

What do you know?	What do you want to know?	What have you learned?
Some people die	How many?	
Some type of treatment	How do you help someone?	
People might have breathing problems	What are the causes?	

FIGURE 6.4

Anticipation Guide
Example: Shock

Directions: Read each statement about shock and choose True or False depending on whether you agree with the statement or disagree.

True	False	Statements About Shock
		Shock can be caused by a heart attack.
		The proper medication is the only treatment for shock.
		Severe diarrhea can cause a person to experience shock.
		Providing fluids is a treatment for shock.

Another way to introduce the content is through an anticipation guide, which provides statements for students to respond to prior to the reading (see Figure 6.4). Herber and Herber (1993) developed this strategy to generate active engagement in the topic and provide a purpose for the reading. After students respond to each statement, the teacher discusses their reactions prior to the introduction of the lesson. This type of guide is a previewing strategy and prompts students to make predictions about what they will be reading. A well-written anticipation guide can motivate students to think more critically about the information to be presented (National Urban Alliance for Effective Education, 2006). Teachers have students revisit this guide after the lesson to validate their responses and to actively engage them in a discussion of the reading.

After introducing the students to what they will be learning, inform them of their responsibilities. This includes class activities and homework that will provide them with the opportunity to interact with the new knowledge, possible projects (formative assessments) that will allow them to demonstrate their understanding of the information, and final (summative) assessments that indicate their competency in using the new knowledge/skills.

MOTIVATION

■ Do some students lack the motivation to learn?
■ Are they more motivated in one subject than in another?

There is a strong correlation between students' motivation levels and their achievement (Willingham, Pollack, & Lewis, 2002). There are many theories about the nature of motivation. While some students actively participate in their learning because they are internally motivated to gain new information and demonstrate their knowledge, others need external motivators. For each student, a teacher may consider tangible reinforcers, such as time to engage in an activity of high interest, a point system attached to individual preferences as positive reinforcement, or elimination of homework responsibility, which is a negative reinforcement. Because not all motivation techniques work for everyone all the time, a teacher might involve students in selecting appropriate ones. As students experience academic success because of the learning environment created, a teacher may find that some students become more involved in their own learning without external motivators.

MONITORING STUDENTS

Considering how to monitor students' progress and provide students with feedback is also part of instructional planning. The use of a spreadsheet or a grading software program provides teachers with formative and summative information, and can be used to

FIGURE 6.5

Grading Software
Websites

www.mistycity.com
www.1st-class-software.com
www.thinkwave.com
www.classbuilder.com
www.rredware.com
www.gradebooks4teachers.com
www.education-world.com/a_tech/tech031.shtml

inform students and parents/guardians about student progress. For some students, the report may provide motivation to improve performance, while for others it provides documentation of their effort and success.

If there is not a schoolwide grading program available and a teacher is not familiar with using spreadsheets, it is worthwhile to explore the Internet sites listed in Figure 6.5 that offer trial editions of grading software to provide the teacher with information to make a judgment about a format that will provide the monitoring information needed.

MNEMONICS

According to Darling-Hammond et al. (2005), students' background knowledge supports their ability to remember new information, but teachers can provide assistance in their ability to retrieve the new information by teaching a mnemonic and having students use it to activate and review the content.

If students are studying the planets, this mnemonic may help them remember the order: *My very excellent mother just sent us nachos.* But the order of the planets is not all that is required in learning about the planets; it is simply the beginning of the understanding. Learning the order provides the students with a basis for understanding additional information about the planets. Figure 6.6 provides more ideas for using mnemonics.

PLANNING FOR ASSESSMENT ALTERNATIVES

According to Mercer and Mercer (2005), assessment should provide the teacher with the data needed to develop an appropriate instructional program. Before selecting how to assess students, review students' IEPs for any testing modifications listed, such as extended time to complete a test or having a test read aloud when the reading may interfere with performance. Look over the records for comments from students' previous teachers about assessment concerns. In choosing the method for students to demonstrate their mastery of the material, decide on whether a written and/or oral assessment is more appropriate. Think about how the students learned the material, their guided practice, and their independent activities. Select a familiar approach to minimize testing anxiety. Because assessment is ongoing (formative), not just summative, use a grading tracking system to provide a complete picture of each student's level of achievement. The way you assess one student may be different from the way you assess another student. Whatever assessment methods are selected need to be valid measures of the objectives being tested.

FIGURE 6.6

Ideas for Mnemonics

Source: Landsberger, Joseph. (December 6, 1998). Using Memory Effectively. *In study guides and strategies.* Retrieved August 4, 2007, from *http://www.studygs.net/ memory/.*

When to Use	Technique
For information involving key words	**Acronym**—An invented combination of letters with each letter acting as a cue to an idea you need to remember.
For information involving key words	**Acrostic**—An invented sentence where the first letter of each word is a cue to an idea you need to remember.
For ordered or unordered lists	**Rhyme-keys**—A two-step memory process: 1. Memorize key words that can be associated with numbers (one-bun). 2. Create an image of the items you need to remember with key words. (A bun with cheese on it will remind me of dairy products.)
For ordered or unordered lists	**Chaining**—Create a story where each word or idea you need to remember will cue the next idea you need to recall.
For approximately 20 items	**Loci method**—Imagine placing the items you want to remember in specific locations in a room with which you are familiar.
For foreign language vocabulary	**Keyword method**—Select the foreign words you need to remember, then identify an English word that sounds like the foreign one. Now imagine an image that involves the key word with the English meaning of the foreign word.
For remembering names	**Image-name technique**—Invents a relationship between the name and the physical characteristics of the person.

For example, one student may need a math problem test read aloud if the reading of the math problems interferes with the student being able to perform the calculations. A reading test cannot be read aloud because that is what is being measured. A teacher should have a discussion with students to help them understand assessment in each subject. Figure 6.7 provides more examples of assessment alternatives that meet student needs.

UNIVERSAL DESIGN FOR LEARNING

Universal design refers to products that are developed for all users, without the need for major adaptations. Universal design calls for multiple means of representation, expression, and engagement (Center for Applied Special Technology, 2007).

Assistive technology that supports individuals with exceptionalities may also be effective for students without exceptionalities by allowing all students various ways of acquiring information, demonstrating their learning, and increasing their involvement in their own learning. An instructional program that incorporates universal design

FIGURE 6.7
Examples of
Assessment
Alternatives: Shock

Student	Summative Assessment
B.J.	Research report using information from text, medical journal, and NIMH Website for five-page report
M.W.	PowerPoint presentation that includes types, causes, and medical interventions along with a student-created fill-in-the-blank test
K.S.	Expository article for a newscast
A.G.	Videotape teaching the main points of shock
R.T.	Oral responses to teacher's questions (one on one)

concepts allows for multiple ways for students to acquire and represent their knowledge, as well as to engage in their learning through technology. Teachers may provide models for approaching assigned tasks, such as templates, outlines, animations, or hyperlinks, to ensure that each student has the support needed to complete the task successfully (Hitchcock, Meyer, Rose, & Jackson, 2002). To make appropriate decisions about how assistive technology (AT) can impact students' success, teachers should stay informed about what services, devices, and software are available for students, along with barriers that may exist in the schools that are preventing access to AT (Edyburn, 2003; Male, 2003). A teaching cycle involves assessing, teaching, and monitoring, so in choosing some form of AT, a teacher needs to have an evaluation of the AT in place to judge its value in helping a student achieve academic goals (Wissick, 2005). A course in assistive technology offers many practical experiences in incorporating technology into teaching to help students achieve. Some students benefit from text-to-speech software, visual organizer software, or some type of writing support software. Some students may need alternative keyboards, switches, or touch screens to make use of the computer. See Figure 6.8 for descriptions of the features of assistive technology.

A district may provide an assistive technology expert to assist teachers in making decisions about using technology for specific students. This person can also provide training for the teacher, the student, and the family.

ACADEMIC LEARNING TIME

Academic learning time refers to the actual time a student is successfully engaged in the content (Berliner, 1990). Developing an effective instructional program based on students' needs, state standards, assessments, engaging lessons, and technology support is part of the teaching process. A teacher needs to understand the strong relationship between the time students are actively engaged in learning and their achievement levels (Brewster & Fager, 2000; Huitt, 2005; Metzker, 2003).

The more class time used by the teacher in involving students in their own learning by ensuring that they are not off task, the more effective is the teaching and learning. A teacher may have a colleague observe a lesson to chart the teacher's and students' engagement in content learning for reflection and analysis purposes. This analysis provides the teacher with data to judge the effectiveness of teaching strategies, classroom management approaches, student groupings, and student learning activities. The coding system in Figure 6.9 is used by an observer to chart teacher's, student's, and overall class behaviors. Take a moment to reflect on successful teaching experiences (see Figure 6.10).

Software Features	Alternative Input
• Easy-to-read screens • Logical labels • Instructional choices • Graphics • Friendly documentation • On-screen instructions • Auditory cues • Visual cues • Built-in access methods • Alternatives to a mouse • Optional cursors • Creation of custom programs	• Switches and switch software • Alternative keyboards • Keyboard additions • Interface devices • Voice recognition • Optical character recognition and scanners • Pointing and typing aids • Touch screens • Joysticks • Trackballs • Arm and wrist supports
Processing Aids	**Alternative Output**
• Abbreviation expansion and macro programs • Word prediction • Talking and large-print word processors • Grammar and spell checkers • Reading comprehension programs • Writing composition programs • Electronic reference tools • Menu management program	• Braille embossers and translators • Refreshable braille displays • Speech synthesizers • Screen readers • Screen-enlargement programs • Monitor additions

FIGURE 6.8

Features of Assistive Technology

Source: Adapted from the Family Guide to Assistive Technology at *http://www.pluk.org/AT1.html#24.*

CONCLUSION

Coursework in curriculum and instruction provides in-depth information on the topics presented in this chapter. The Websites and References at the end of this chapter offer resources to assist your instructional planning. Successful teachers strengthen their knowledge about planning instruction through study and reflection of the teaching process to improve the learning environment for students.

"You learn at your best when you have something you care about and can get pleasure in being engaged in."

Howard Gardner

EXPLORATIONS

1. Review the section in this chapter on background knowledge. Develop an anticipation guide for a lesson that you are planning to teach. After using the anticipation guide, reflect on the process. Did this guide help to promote active engagement of your students in the lesson? The next time you develop an anticipation guide, what would you do differently? What would remain the same?
2. What role might technology have in the classroom to promote active learning? Visit several of the suggested Websites to develop ideas on how incorporating technology into teaching and learning can enhance the instructional program. Develop a sample lesson incorporating technology.

FIGURE 6.9

Academic Learning
Time

Teacher Behaviors

OP	Organization, plan
PI	Provide instruction
PE	Provide further explanations
OA	Observe academics (checks work)
AQ	Ask questions of pupils
PAF	Provide academic feedback
OT	Observe to see if pupils are on task
PBF	Provide behavior feedback
NI	Not interacting with pupils

Class Behaviors

FT	Free time
CB	Class business
NCA	Noncontent activities
T	Transition
NA	No activity, pupils

Targeted Student Behaviors

SQ	Student questions
SS	Student speaking
SW	Student writing
SLE	Student looks engaged
SGD	Student getting directions
SGR	Student getting ready
SNH	Student needs help
SOT	Student off task

Think About	Reflect	Respond
Experiences working with students	Discuss experiences where you felt successful working with students.	
Experiences observing effective teachers	What contributed to these teachers being successful with their students?	
	Describe each teacher's instructional program.	
Experiences working or observing students obviously very engaged in their learning	Discuss the learning environment of these students.	
	What contributed to their being so engaged?	

FIGURE 6.10

Take a Moment

3. Read about academic learning time on the Internet. How might you increase students' time on task to actively engage them in their learning? Tape yourself teaching to provide you with insights on how you and the students are spending class time.
4. Look over students' IEPs to familiarize yourself with the information that was collected to document their exceptionalities. Create a chart listing each of the students along with the specific information that provides instructional programming ideas based on their needs.
5. Work with one of the grading programs to familiarize yourself with how it works. Discuss the various types of printouts that might be helpful to present the progress of your students to them and their parents/guardians.
6. List ideas for how you can improve the learning environment of students.

WEBSITES

CAST Universal Design for Learning
http://www.cast.org/research/udl/
This site suggests ways a teacher using universal design concepts can address various exceptionalities.

Closing the Gap
http://www.closingthegap.com
This site provides information on technology for persons with disabilities.

Family Guide to Assistive Technology
http://www.pluk.org/AT1.html#24
This site offers information on the various features of assistive technology.

Microsoft Office Online
http://office.microsoft.com/en-us/FX011595351033.aspx?mode=print
This site offers information and provides templates for incorporating technology into teaching.

North Central Regional Educational Laboratory
http://www.ncrel.org/sdrs/areas/issues/methods/technlgy/te1000.htm
This site discusses the components of a professional development plan on technology.

University of Texas at Austin, Division of Instructional Innovation and Assessment
http://www.utexas.edu/academic/diia/assessment/iar/resources/best_practices/index.php
This site provides an overview of best practices and steps on how to incorporate technology into teaching.

REFERENCES

Berliner, D. (1990). What's all the fuss about instructional time? Retrieved February 27, 2006 from: *http://courses.ed.asu.edu/berliner/readings/fuss/fuss.htm.*

Brewster, C., & Fager, J. (2000). *Increasing student engagement and motivation: From time-on-task to homework.* Retrieved January 2, 2001 from *http://www.nwrel.org/request/oct00/textonly.html.*

Center for Applied Special Technology. (2007). Universal design for learning. Retrieved June 9, 2007 from *http://www.cast.org/research/edu.*

Darling-Hammond, L., Banks, J., Zumwalt, K., Gomez, L., Sherin, M., Griesdorn, J., & Finn, L. (2005). Theories of learning and their roles in teaching. In L. Darling-Hammond & J. Bransford (Eds.), *Preparing teachers for a changing world* (pp. 40–87). California: Jossey-Bass.

Edyburn, D. (2003). *What every teacher should know about assistive technology.* Boston: Allyn & Bacon.

Herber, H., & Herber, J. (1993). *Teaching in content areas with reading, writing, and reasoning.* Boston: Allyn & Bacon.

Hitchcock, C., Meyer, A., Rose, D., & Jackson, R. (2002). Providing access to the new general curriculum. *Teaching Exceptional Children, 35*(2), 8–17.

Huitt, W. (2005). Academic learning time. *Educational Psychology Interactive.* Valdosta, GA: Valdosta State University. Retrieved May 1, 2005 from *http://chiron.valdosta. edu/whuitt/col/process/ALT.html.*

Male, M. (2003). *Technology for inclusion: Meeting the special needs of all students.* Boston: Allyn & Bacon.

Marzano, R. (2003). *What works in schools: Translating research into action.* Virginia: Association for Supervision and Curriculum Development.

Mercer, C., & Mercer, A. (2005). *Teaching students with learning problems.* Upper Saddle River, NJ: Merrill/Prentice Hall.

Metzker, B. (2003). Time and learning. Retrieved December 10, 2003 from *http://eric. uoregon.edu/publications/digests/digest166.html.*

National and Community Service Act of 1990. (Title 1, Sub-title B, Section 3).

National Urban Alliance for Effective Education. (2006). Retrieved March 20, 2006 from *http://www.nuatc.org/resources/strategy/cogstrat.html.*

Orlich, D. C., Harder, R., Callahan, R., & Gibson, H. (2001). *Teaching strategies: A guide to better instruction.* Boston: Houghton Mifflin.

Powell, W., & Napoliello, S. (2005). Using observation to improve instruction. *Educational Leadership, 62*(5), 52–55.

Slavin, R. (2006). *Educational psychology* (8th ed.). Boston: Pearson/Allyn & Bacon.

Willingham, W. W., Pollack, J. M., & Lewis, C. (2002). Grades and test scores: Accounting for observed differences. *Journal of Educational Measurement 39*(1): 1–37.

Wissick, C. (2005). Written language: When to consider technology. *Technology in Action, 1*(6), 1–12.

Ysseldyke, S. (2004). *Assessment in special and inclusion education.* MA: Houghton Mifflin.

7

Instructional Strategies

"There's a great differentiated instruction analogy in a scene from Rodgers and Hammerstein's movie, The Sound of Music. *At one point, Maria Von Trapp (Julie Andrews) takes the seven children on a bike ride. As they ride, some children follow the teacher, some ride alongside the teacher, and some move ahead. One is carried piggyback style on Maria's back because she can't ride at all. Despite everyone's different rate and competency with bike riding, the group is moving as a whole; everyone is on the trip, advanced and struggling bike riders, and no one is left behind. The teacher scaffolded the instruction for some of them, and she allowed the more advanced children to surpass the teacher in execution of the skill."*

Wormelli, 2003

Chapter Objectives

- Discuss teacher-directed strategies
- Review cooperative group strategies
- Provide information and resources on service learning

Before you read this chapter, think about the instructional strategies with which you are familiar. Have you had success with one more than the others? Have you thought about why? How involved have the students been in their own learning? Record your reflections and revisit your response as you read this chapter.

Introduction

Curriculum design, classroom management, and effective instruction are considered the most important factors that contribute to student achievement (Marzano, Gaddy, & Dean, 2000). There is no one teaching strategy appropriate for all content, at all grade levels, with all students, all the time. Teachers consider the developmental levels of the students, their abilities and needs, the curriculum objectives, and student outcomes when choosing an instructional strategy (Wiles & Bondi, 2007). Teachers then adapt the strategy to differentiate instruction to provide the environment where students can experience success. Teachers vary the pacing of the lesson, facilitate grouping for different needs, and provide a variety of independent activities (multimodality responses), including technology as a support. This chapter highlights several instructional strategies.

Teacher-Directed Strategies

Explicit Teaching

In the explicit teaching strategy, the teacher creates a very structured environment when introducing a new topic or teaching a new skill. In explicit teaching (Slavin, 2006), the teacher presents the lesson objective, ensures that students have the background knowledge needed to understand the new material, presents the new material, monitors the students

FIGURE 7.1

Direct Instruction

Source: From Bruce
Joyce, Marsha Weil, &
Emily Calhoun, *Models of
Teaching, Mylabschool
Edition,* 7/e. Published by
Allyn and Bacon, Boston,
MA. Copyright © 2004 by
Pearson Education.
Adapted by permission of
the author.

1. *Objectives:* behavior/performance objectives are stated.
2. *Standards:* align objectives with standards.
3. *Anticipatory set:* create a type of organizer to focus attention.
4. *Teaching:* provide information through lectures, examples, visuals, and problem-solving experiences.
5. *Guided practice:* supervise students as they practice new learning.
6. *Closure:* review and clarify students' understanding.
7. *Independent practice:* provide opportunities for students to gain understanding.

FIGURE 7.2

Sample Concept
Development Model

Process	Students' Responses
List	Generate a list based on topic or questions presented by teacher.
Group	Use list to categorize items based on what belongs together.
Label	Develop labels for each of the groups.
Synthesize	Summarize the information and make generalizations.

engaged in an activity to promote learning of the objective, and assesses the students in independent practice demonstrating their learning. The teacher models the behavior and skill that is being taught through demonstrations and guiding the students in their responses (Carnine, Silbert, Kame'enui, & Tarver, 2004). This strategy can be easily adapted depending on the ages and needs of the students along with the demands of the content.

When collaborating with general education teachers who use this strategy, the special education teacher should first observe the class to consider any modifications that might contribute to students' success in this instructional environment, and then collaborate with the general education teacher to develop an instructional plan. Figure 7.1 summarizes the direct instruction method.

CONCEPT DEVELOPMENT TEACHING

The concept development strategy works well when the teacher's goal is to introduce and extend students' understanding of a specific concept through analyzing examples and data (Gunter, Estes, & Mintz, 2007). The teacher introduces the lesson by guiding the students in a discussion of what is already known and understood about the concept, and identifying positive and negative examples of the concept. As students list what they associate with the topic, they create categories of terms as a way of deepening their understanding of the concept. Students then discuss their broadened understanding of the concept and investigate new relationships using the concept. Figure 7.2 provides a sample of concept development strategies.

COOPERATIVE LEARNING STRATEGIES

In establishing cooperative groups, the teacher considers the strengths and needs of the students along with a variety of materials required for each student to successfully achieve the desired outcome. For students who are not familiar with how to work in cooperative groups, the teacher may conduct a simulation to ensure productive outcomes.

Assigning specific roles in the groups will allow students to develop independence and interdependence with their own learning. Working in small groups provides students the opportunity to work with and learn from classmates to achieve a specific learning outcome. There are many different types of cooperative groups, so it is important to consider the purpose and advantage of each type. This chapter provides examples of two types of groups: Jigsaw and reciprocal teaching.

JIGSAW STRATEGY

The jigsaw strategy involves creating expert groups that are responsible for one aspect of the subject being studied. This technique is used for nonlinear learning, such as understanding the food groups, the organs of the body, or weather terms. Whatever each small group is studying to report on to the whole class is not dependent on the knowledge another group has for understanding the content. Before using this technique, an overview of the content to be researched is presented to ensure that students have the background information necessary to scaffold more in-depth content. The teacher selects the specific activities for each student based on their instructional needs and their IEP objectives. The teacher selects the groups and provides the materials based on each student's ability to read/write and respond to content. The idea is that each small group becomes an expert in one area and then shares the information with the whole group in a variety of ways (posters, video, PowerPoint, panel, etc.). The teacher arranges the presentation of the content to facilitate the students' understanding of the whole subject. The goal is to facilitate your students' academic achievement through this approach. Figure 7.3 shows a Jigsaw approach to a social studies project.

RECIPROCAL TEACHING

Another type of cooperative grouping is called reciprocal teaching (Palincsar & Brown, 1984). Consider this strategy when working with expository material. After the teacher models for students how to summarize information, create questions, clarify understanding, and make predictions, the students work in groups to study text material so that they can become the experts in leading a discussion—an active role that promotes dialogue with classmates and the teacher. The teacher can assess the students' understanding of the material by listening to the questions they generate, their responses to other students, how they clarify information, and their summaries. Figure 7.4 lists the four aspects of reciprocal teaching.

FIGURE 7.3

Jigsaw Strategy Example

Steps	Social Studies Assignment: World Religions
Teacher forms cooperative groups (expert groups)	Assigns each group one religion to study history and beliefs.
Expert groups' tasks	Read, discuss material, and prepare a presentation for class.
Whole-group reporting	Expert groups report on major findings. Whole group demonstrates understanding.

FIGURE 7.4

Reciprocal Teaching

Source: From "Thinking Aloud and Reading Comprehension Research: Inquiry, Instruction, and Social Interaction," by L. Kucan & I. Beck, 1997, *Review of Educational Research, 67*(3), 281. Reprinted with permission.

In reciprocal teaching the teacher and the students take turns assuming the role of teacher by engaging the group in a dialogue. This structured dialogue includes these four strategies:

- Asking questions
- Clarifying points
- Summarizing text
- Making predictions

SERVICE LEARNING

Special education teachers are challenged daily by the unique needs of their students. As educators, we are constantly searching for instructional strategies that address the specific needs of our students while providing meaningful and appropriate experiences that stimulate their interest in learning and address state educational standards. Service learning, a method of learning and teaching, has the potential to meet these instructional challenges. By definition, service learning is:

> . . . a way of teaching and learning that actively involves the students through service to their communities. In addition to fostering civic responsibility and individual development, service learning allows the students to participate and learn through meaningful activities. (National and Community Service Act, 1990)

The seven elements of a high-quality service learning program, according to the Service Learning Center (2000), are: (1) integrated learning experience, (2) active student voice, (3) high-quality service, (4) civic responsibility, (5) collaboration, (6) reflection, and (7) evaluation. A brief description of these elements and how they may specifically benefit children with exceptionalities follows.

INTEGRATED LEARNING

- The service learning project has clearly articulated knowledge, skill, or value goals that arise from broader classroom or school goals.
- The service informs the academic learning content, and the academic learning content informs the service.
- Life skills learned outside the classroom are integrated into classroom learning.

Potential Benefits for Students with Exceptional Needs

- Provides students with an opportunity to generalize classroom concepts into the broader community.

STUDENT VOICE

Students participate actively in:

- Choosing and planning the service project.
- Planning and implementing the reflection sessions, evaluations, and celebrations.
- Taking on roles and tasks that are appropriate to their age.

Potential Benefits for Students with Exceptional Needs

▓ Targets age-appropriate tasks that are often overlooked in special education classrooms.
▓ Provides students with the opportunity to select areas of study that are of interest to them and promotes meaningful learning.

HIGH-QUALITY SERVICE

▓ The service responds to an actual community need that is recognized by the community.
▓ The service is age appropriate and well organized.
▓ The service is designed to achieve significant benefits for students and the community.

Potential Benefits for Students with Exceptional Needs

▓ Encourages awareness of others' needs.

CIVIC RESPONSIBILITY

▓ The service learning project promotes students' responsibility to care for others and to contribute to the community.
▓ By participating in the service learning project, students understand how they can impact their community.

Potential Benefits for Students with Exceptional Needs

▓ Fosters a sense of empowerment, which can often be missing in the lives of students with exceptionalities.

COLLABORATION

▓ The service learning project is a collaboration among as many of these partners as is feasible: parents, community-based organizations, staff, school administrators, teachers, and recipients of the service.
▓ All partners benefit from the project and contribute to its planning.

Potential Benefits for Students with Exceptional Needs

▓ Promotes opportunities for students with social challenges to work as team members and enhances social interaction skills.

REFLECTION

▓ Reflection establishes connections between students' service experiences and the academic curriculum.
▓ Reflection occurs before, during, and after the service learning project.

Potential Benefits for Students with Exceptional Needs

▓ Encourages higher levels of thinking that may not be emphasized in alternate curriculum approaches.

FIGURE 7.5

Service Learning
Websites

> **Learn and Serve**
> *http://www.learnandserve.org*
>
> **Youth Service America**
> *http://www.ysa.org*
>
> **Students in Service to America**
> *http://www.studentsinservicetoamerica.org*
>
> **Council for Exceptional Children**
> *http://www.cec.sped.org*

FIGURE 7.6

Take a Moment

Think About	Reflect	Respond
Experiences with instructional strategies	What strategies do you use more than others? Why?	
Strategies that engage the students	What strategies seem to engage the students more in their own learning?	
Assessment results	Is there a correlation between teaching strategies and student performance? Explain.	

EVALUATION

■ All the partners, especially students, are involved in evaluating the service learning project.

■ The evaluation seeks to measure progress toward the learning goals of the project.

Potential benefits for students with exceptional needs

■ Students are encouraged to take responsibility for their own learning; fosters self-assessment.

Service learning is viewed as a viable and practical instructional strategy for motivating students with exceptional needs. Figure 7.5 lists Websites that offer more information on service learning, and Figure 7.6 asks you to reflect on the instructional strategies covered in this chapter.

CONCLUSION

This chapter reviewed several instructional strategies as a way to prompt you to reflect on your teaching and the active engagement of your students in their own learning. Effective teachers create positive learning environments by selecting instructional strategies based on their students' needs and the demands of the curriculum.

EXPLORATIONS

1. Reflect on a lesson taught where students did not experience success. Rethink how to teach the lesson so that students' needs and content demands are met. What would be different in the revised lesson?
2. Collaborate with colleagues in planning a lesson. Discuss how students' strengths and weaknesses need to be addressed in selecting an instructional strategy.
3. Observe a colleague who teaches a diverse group of learners who experience success. What strategies are employed?
4. Discuss with students the type of active learning they feel assists them in understanding the content. Review their informal and formal assessments. Is there a correlation between how they like to learn and their achievement levels?

WEBSITES

Basic Lesson Presentation Elements
http://www.humboldt.edu/~tha1/hunter-eei.html
This site provides detailed information on the elements of effective instruction.

Glossary of Instructional Strategies
http://glossary.plasmalink.com/glossary.html
This site provides links to hundreds of methods teachers might use.

Instructional Strategies Online
http://olc.spsd.sk.ca/DE/PD/instr/alpha.html
This site provides an alphabetical list of instructional methods.

Learning Theories and Instructional Strategies Matrix
http://www.kihd.gmu.edu/immersion/knowledgebase/
This site links instructional strategies with learning theories.

Mid-Continent Research for Education and Learning
http://www.mcrel.org/Newsroom/hottopicInstruction.asp
This site provides a chart listing instructional practices associated with higher levels of student achievement.

The Middle Web Listserv
http://www.middleweb.com/MWLresources/marzchat1.html
This site identifies Marzano's nine instructional strategies.

REFERENCES

Barry, A. (2002). Reading strategies teachers say they use. *Journal of Adolescent & Adult Literacy, 46*(2), 132–141.

Carnine, D., Silbert, J., Kame'enui, E., & Tarver, S. (2004). *Direct instruction reading.* Upper Saddle River, NJ: Merrill/Prentice Hall.

Guerin, G., & Male, M. C. (2006). *Addressing learning disabilities and difficulties: How to reach and teach every student.* Thousand Oaks, CA: Corwin Press.

Gunter, M., Estes, T., & Mintz, S. (2007) *Instruction: A model approach.* Boston: Allyn & Bacon.

Hall, T. (2002). *Explicit instruction.* Wakefield, MA: National Center on Accessing the General Curriculum. Retrieved November 1, 2006 from *http://www.cast.org/publications/ncac/ncac_explicit.html.*

Huitt, W. (2005). Direct instruction: A transactional model. *Educational Psychology Interactive*. Valdosta, GA: Valdosta State University. Retrieved November 1, 2006 from *http://chiron.valdosta.edu/whuitt/col/instruct/dirinst.html*.

Learning Disabilities Association. (2006). Response to intervention model (RTI). Retrieved February 27, 2006 from *http://www.ldonline.org/ld_indepth/assessment/response_to_intervention.html*.

Marzano, R. J., Gaddy, B. B., & Dean, C. (2000). *What works in classroom instruction*. Aurora, CO: Mid-continent Research for Education and Learning.

Mellard, D. (2005). Understanding responsiveness to intervention in learning disabilities. Retrieved April 1, 2006 from *http://nrcld.org/publications/papers/mallard.shtml*.

National and Community Service Act of 1990: As amended through December 17, 1999, P. L. 106-170. Retrieved June 10, 2007 from *http://www.csc.ca.gov/aboutus/documents/ncsa1990.pdf*.

Orligh, D., Harder, R., Callahan, R., & Gibson, H. (2001). *Teaching strategies: A guide to better instruction*. New York: Houghton Mifflin.

Palincsar, A. S., & Brown, A. L. (1984). Reciprocal teaching of comprehension-fostering and comprehension-monitoring activities. *Cognition and Instruction, 1*(2), 117–175.

Service-Learning Center. (2000). Retrieved June 10, 2007 from Service-Learning Project Assessment Tool from *http://www.psdschools.org/documentlibrary/downloads/partnerships.Volunteers/Sl.Project_Assessment_Tool.pdf*.

Slavin, R. (2006). *Educational psychology* (8th ed.). Boston: Pearson/Allyn & Bacon.

Wiles, J., & Bondi, J. (2007). *Curriculum development: A guide to practice*. Upper Saddle River, NJ: Prentice Hall.

Wormeli, R. (2003). Differentiating instruction: A modified concerto in four movements. Retrieved January 2005 from *http://www.ldonline.org/ld_indepth/teaching_techniques/modified_concerto.html*.

Supervision of Paraprofessionals

"Alone we can do so little; together we can do so much."

Helen Keller

CHAPTER OBJECTIVES

- Describe paraprofessional responsibilities
- Present strategies for clarifying classroom roles and responsibilities
- Provide a user-friendly process for implementing a paraprofessional needs assessment
- Discuss how to establish a positive working environment
- Present practical activities for creating an open communication system
- Discuss steps to manage conflict
- Provide a checklist to evaluate the special education teacher/paraprofessional team process

> *Before reading this chapter, consider what comes to mind when you think of working with your paraprofessional. What are your expectations of the paraprofessional? Are both of your roles understood? How can you improve the working environment so that you and your paraprofessional work as a team in the classroom? Record your reflections and revisit your response as you read this chapter.*

INTRODUCTION

More than one special education teacher has been humbled by the powerful impact of a paraprofessional in his or her classroom. The professional relationship that is established early on in the school year can set the stage for months of positive and productive teamwork, or result in a year of frustration and unproductive expenditures of time and energy.

This chapter addresses key strategies and processes to ensure a productive and rewarding working relationship between you and the paraprofessionals with whom you work. The strategies will help you establish the working environment, implement a needs assessment, establish roles and responsibilities, foster open communication, and evaluate the teacher/paraprofessional team process.

DESCRIPTION OF PARAPROFESSIONAL RESPONSIBILITIES

Paraprofessionals can be referred to by a variety titles: aides, teacher aides, teaching assistants, educational assistants, instructional assistants and paraeducators. Paraprofessionals are individuals who provide instructional assistance to teachers, allowing teachers to focus their attention on instructional planning and teaching. Paraprofessionals are employed to provide enrichment, encouragement, and support to students in their daily activities (Bureau of Labor Statistics, 2005).

Fifty years ago, when paraprofessionals were first introduced into the nation's school systems, much of their job responsibilities centered around providing teachers with additional time to develop and implement curriculum. Their responsibilities included performing routine clerical tasks, monitoring students during nonacademic activities, and reinforcing lessons given by the teacher. Over the last 20 years research has shown that a majority of paraprofessionals are now engaged in a variety of complex activities that center around assisting teachers in instruction and providing direct instructional services to students and families (Gaylord, Wallace, Pickett, & Litkins, 2002). Currently, one of the most common support strategies used in the general education classroom for students with disabilities is to assign a paraprofessional or an instructional assistant (Crutchfield, 1997) to work one-on-one with the student (Causton-Theoharis & Malmgren, 2005).

Although there is no definitive list of paraprofessional responsibilities, the following provides teachers with a description of appropriate responsibilities:

- Engage individual and small groups of learners in activities in classrooms and community-based settings.
- Carry out behavior management and disciplinary plans developed by teachers.
- Assist teachers with functional assessments and other assessments activities.
- Document and provide objective information about learner performance that enables teachers to plan lessons and modify curriculum content and instructional activities to meet the needs of individual learners.
- Assist teachers with organizing and maintaining supportive, safe learning environments.
- Assist teachers with involving parents or other caregivers in their child's education.
- Assist nurses, physical therapists, and speech-language pathologists with providing services required by learners with physical, speech, language, and sensory disabilities and chronic health-care needs.
- Participate as required in meetings to develop individual education plans, individual family service plans, and individual transition plans. (Pickett, 2002, p. 2).

You, as the special education teacher, are responsible for all planning of instruction and management in your classroom. Keeping this in mind, your paraprofessional should not be asked to perform the following activities:

- Plan instruction
- Diagnose disabilities
- Prescribe interventions
- Evaluate academic or behavioral performance
- Select learning materials and/or equipment
- Supervise students on field trips without a teacher

Before engaging in a joint discussion of job responsibilities, it is vital for you to have a clear understanding of the criteria on which your school districts paraprofessional evaluation is based. Nothing is more disconcerting for a paraprofessional than to be evaluated on one set of criteria established by the teacher and then find out that another set of criteria is being used for retaining employment. Before a discussion of roles and responsibilities, we recommend that you acquire a copy of the paraprofessional's employment evaluation and use the criteria listed as guidelines for designating your paraprofessional's instructional roles and responsibilities. We also suggest that your paraprofessional receive a blank copy of the school district's evaluation form at the beginning of the school year, and that you thoroughly review the form with your paraprofessional, giving ample time for questions and clarification regarding the criteria for evaluation.

STRATEGIES FOR CLARIFYING CLASSROOM ROLES AND RESPONSIBILITIES

It is important that roles and responsibilities be thoroughly discussed with your paraprofessional before she or he assumes responsibility for each task assigned. Having the opportunity to clearly define each instructional task and clarify who is responsible for implementing the task will work preventatively in addressing issues of control, self-esteem, and role confusion. Clearly designating both of your responsibilities in writing is paramount in preventing role confusion and frustration. Figure 8.1 provides an example of a user-friendly form to help you clarify and document, in writing, the roles and job responsibilities for both you and your paraprofessional.

Task	Paraprofessional	Teacher
Weekly planning		X
Explanation of lesson plans		X
Implementing lesson plans	X	X
Informing parents of IEP meetings		X
Discussing behavioral or instructional concerns with parents		X
Developing and monitoring IEP goals and objectives		X
Assessing and recording IEP progress		X
Charting student performance	X	X
Consulting with support services		X
Assisting students in inclusive settings	X	X
Assisting students in task completion	X	X
Developing agenda items for paraprofessional meetings	X	X
Scheduling and facilitating paraprofessional meetings		X
Constructing instructional materials developed by teacher	X	X
Assisting students' arrival and departure on bus	X	X
Determining content of bulletin boards		X
Constructing bulletin boards	X	
Assisting in toileting and positioning	X	X

FIGURE 8.1

Roles and Responsibilities Clarification

Source: Adapted from Dr. Hsuying Ward. (2005). California State University, Chico. Chico, CA.

FIGURE 8.2

Take a Moment

Think About	Reflect	Respond
Roles and responsibilities	How can clear roles and responsibilities help your paraprofessional in the classroom?	

Misunderstanding of the roles and responsibilities between teachers and paraprofessionals has led many classrooms to dissolve under a cloud of chaos and dysfunction. In a recent study, it was determined that differences in perception of job roles and responsibilities can lead to incongruent expectations and misunderstandings between teachers and paraprofessionals (Wallace, Shin, Bartholomay, & Stahl, 2001). These researchers advise that differences in perceptions should be clarified "through the development of relevant job descriptions, regular planning, and ongoing communication between teachers and paraprofessionals" (p. 529). Figure 8.2 asks you to reflect on rotes and responsibilities.

IMPLEMENTATION OF A NEEDS ASSESSMENT

In the hectic days leading up to preparing for a new school year, it is easy to understand why beginning special education teachers often move ahead quickly to establish the logistical aspects of their paraprofessional's roles and responsibilities. This zealousness, however, can often be counterproductive if you and your paraprofessional have contradictory expectations of the instructional and managerial responsibilities (Wallace et al., 2001). By comparing and contrasting your paraprofessional's work preferences with your expectations as the special education teacher, you establish a foundation for open communication that supports effective teaching throughout the academic year (Pickett, 2002). We suggest using a paraprofessional needs assessment to provide a foundation for this communication.

Before implementing a paraprofessional needs assessment, it is important for you to understand why you are asking for your paraprofessional's feedback, how the feedback will be used, and who will have access to the feedback. For this information to be candid and useful, your paraprofessional needs to be assured that the feedback provided is confidential and will not be used as a means of performance evaluation, nor will it be seen as a personal affront to you, as the teacher.

It is often helpful for you and your paraprofessional to have a vehicle by which both of you can compare individual learning styles, values, and work habit preferences (see Figure 8.3).

After independently completing this activity, you and your paraprofessional can discuss your responses and explore ways in which you both can accommodate each other's styles. This candid discussion can pave the way to an honest exploration of the strengths and needs of each team member and can help lay the foundation for defining role responsibilities that mutually benefit the instructional team and, ultimately, your students. Figure 8.4 shows a sample needs assessment.

Providing your paraprofessional with an opportunity to openly express individual strengths and needs in classroom management, instruction, and communication will also enhance student learning (see Figure 8.5).

Figures 8.4 and 8.5 provide you with conversational tools to address individual gaps in your paraprofessional's understanding of classroom instruction, management, and

Comparing Individual
Preferences

Compare the four pairs of statements below. Place a checkmark beside the one statement in each pair that best describes you.

Group One

A. _____ I enjoy working with others and I share my experiences and opinions readily.

B. _____ I prefer working alone and often feel shy in expressing my opinions in group settings.

Group Two

A. _____ I enjoy tasks that can be completed quickly and do not require a lot of prior thought or preparation.

B. _____ I enjoy tasks that have multiple steps and appreciate thorough and clear instructions on the preparation of the task.

Group Three

A. _____ I respond well to spontaneous interruptions and appreciate variety in the tasks I'm given.

B. _____ I respond well to routine and find satisfaction in earning how to do a task well.

Group Four

A. _____ I tend to solve problems by exploring the logical steps needed to address the issue.

B. _____ I tend to solve problems by exploring all the reasons that may have led up to the problem and then determining multiple possibilities for solving the issue.

After selecting one preference in each of the four groups, compare and contrast your choices with your instructional partner(s). Discuss how the similarities and differences in your preferences may affect your efforts to work together as an instructional team. Also explore ways that your preferences may complement and balance out each other's strengths and needs. Discuss how these differences may need to be accommodated.

communication skills. This information is pivotal in providing guidelines for the development of appropriate paraprofessional training. It is interesting to note that approximately 70% to 90% of paraprofessionals are hired without prior training (Crutchfield, 1997). A comprehensive training program can help a paraprofessional become more effective, positive, and empowered (Twachtman-Cullen, 1998). Giangreco and Broer (2005) strongly support that paraprofessionals need a knowledge base of different forms of classroom instructional strategies when working with students and should be included in all training that provides access to this information. The paraprofessional needs analysis provided in this chapter will assist you in determining the type of training that will benefit your paraprofessional.

In addition, you will be alerted to the areas in which your paraprofessional feels most adept. Building on these strengths and needs will complement the individual differences you and your paraprofessional bring to the classroom.

Chapter 8

FIGURE 8.4

Paraprofessional
Needs Assessment

Source: Adapted from
Pickett, 2002.

Please review each responsibility and note whether you feel comfortable with this task or whether you would benefit from more information or training in this role. Note your specific strengths and/or needs in each area of responsibility.

Responsibilities	I understand how to accomplish this job responsibility	I would benefit from more information and/or training
Engage individuals and small groups of students in instructional activities		
Carry out behavioral management and disciplinary plans		
Assist teacher with functional and other assessment activities		
Document and provide objective information about student performance		
Assist teacher with organizing and maintaining positive and supportive learning environments		
Assist teacher in involving parents or caregivers in their child's education		
Participate in required meetings to develop individual education plans, individual family plans, an individual transition plans		

ESTABLISHMENT OF A POSITIVE WORKING ENVIRONMENT

When examining the necessary elements for the successful supervision of paraprofessionals, it is important to remember that the classroom represents a group of adults and children who bring a myriad of personalities and experiences into the mix of everyday interactions and activities. Before delving into the intricacies of these dynamics and how they affect successful collaboration between teachers and paraprofessionals, it is important to consider the essential components of establishing a working environment that supports efficiency of instruction and acknowledges the importance of personal space.

According to noted psychologist Abraham Maslow, certain basic physical and emotional human needs must be addressed before people can focus on higher levels of growth and self-actualization (Norwood, 1996). When considering the hours a paraprofessional

FIGURE 8.5
Paraprofessional
Needs Assessment

The most challenging part of my job is:

I think I could do my job better if:

I think implementation of classroom rules and behavioral techniques in this program are:

_____ consistent, _____ not consistent

My job description is: _____ clear, _____ not clear

Aspects of my job that need clarification are:

I would appreciate more training with:

____ math and reading strategies

____ computer software

____ aggressive, defiant behavior

____ off-task behavior

____ other:

I feel least able to help _____ (student's name) because:

Additional ideas that might help me become a more effective instructional team member:

spends weekly in the classroom environment, it is apparent why addressing these basic physiological and psychological needs should become the first priority in establishing an effective instructional environment.

PHYSIOLOGICAL NEEDS

Physiological needs represent the most basic of human needs for physical comfort and include such essentials as food, water, and rest. When establishing an instructional schedule for paraprofessionals, we recommend that you, as the special education teacher, be aware of the need for consistent scheduled breaks. We also suggest that you become acquainted with your district's contracted times for the paraprofessional's working hours and scheduled breaks.

Paraprofessionals new to the school site should be given a tour of the school campus and shown the location of the staff room, adult restrooms, and other essential facilities, including appropriate parking.

PSYCHOLOGICAL NEEDS

Another basic human need is the need to feel safe and secure. When welcoming your paraprofessional into the classroom it is important to provide him or her with a sense of stability and consistency. It is essential that your paraprofessional be provided a secure, locked place for personal items. This secure place can be a specific drawer in a locked file cabinet, a locked closet, or any other space that can be accessed solely by the paraprofessional.

Human beings have an innate desire to feel accepted and appreciated by others. We convey appreciation and respect for each other in a variety of ways. One tangible way you can convey that your paraprofessional is an important member of the instructional team is by providing a designated instructional space for work and materials, even if it is only a small table.

The fundamental need for feeling competent and being recognized for our abilities plays an important role in the interpersonal dynamics between special education teachers and paraprofessionals. Working in special education classrooms can be challenging. Paraprofessionals assume multiple roles and often work long days.

If you are able to demonstrate appreciation of your paraprofessional's special skills and attributes, you will foster a partnership based on mutual respect and concern. This appreciation can be shown through a variety of ways based on the individual preference of each paraprofessional:

- Write a personal thank-you card.
- Submit a letter of commendation to the school administrator for placement in the paraprofessional's personnel file.
- Treat the paraprofessional to lunch.
- Help your students write a letter or create a video of appreciation for your paraprofessional.

CREATION OF AN OPEN COMMUNICATION SYSTEM

Establishing a positive physiological and psychological environment, determining the strengths and needs of your paraprofessional, and examining your paraprofessional's roles and responsibilities all contribute to providing clear lines of communication between you and your paraprofessional. It is also important to remember that maintaining clear communication is an ongoing process that takes time. Additionally, a shared belief that the effort will lead to the establishment of a more enjoyable and productive learning environment for students will help to foster open communication between you and your paraprofessional.

VALUE OF EFFECTIVE COMMUNICATION

A recent research study (Wallace et al., 2001) surveyed paraprofessionals, teachers, and administrators to determine what competencies and skills they felt were required of teachers to effectively supervise paraprofessionals. All three groups listed

FIGURE 8.6
Ten Tips for Effective
Communication

1	Use positively worded statements versus negative statements: "I know we can all come to agreement" versus "We need to stop arguing!"
2	Listen with empathy. Allow speakers to express their own views without judging their responses.
3	Be assertive. Using "I" rather than "you" statements allows the speaker to state his or her feelings without disregarding concern for the other person. For example, "I need time to think about what you just said" versus "You are pressuring me to make a decision."
4	Reflect on and avoid words or responses that trigger anger, defensiveness, frustration, or sorrow. For example, "Direct instruction is the only way these students will be able to learn."
5	Remember that nonverbal language (how you position your body, eye contact, nodding your head, etc.) is as powerful a communication tool as verbal language.
6	Conflict resolution can follow one of three paths: I win, you lose; you win, I lose; I win, you win. Always choose win/win.
7	It's hard to argue with someone who doesn't argue back.
8	Develop and follow a classroom plan for dealing with professional and personal conflicts.
9	Take time to build positive relationships that are based on parity and a respect for individual strengths and diversity.
10	Never feel rushed to make an important decision or response: "I know how important this decision is and I want to make sure I give it enough thought. I will discuss this with you tomorrow."

communication as being among one of the top teacher skills needed for supervising paraprofessionals. It is essential for teachers to be able to express themselves clearly and to be able to accurately interpret information and emotions. Figure 8.6 provides 10 tips to foster effective communication.

SIX BASIC ACTIVE LISTENING TECHNIQUES

Six basic active listening techniques can be used to facilitate communication: encouraging, clarifying, restating, reflecting, summarizing, and validating. When used effectively by teachers, these techniques can help paraprofessionals express their thoughts and feelings and help teachers glean important information (Eagan, 1982). These techniques may also help teachers sort through a variety of interpersonal issues that may be standing in the way of clear communication and productive teamwork in the classroom.

Because effective communication is a complex skill that takes considerable study and practice, it is not the purpose of this section to provide you a lengthy description of the six techniques. Instead, a quick reference chart has been provided in Figure 8.7 that summarizes the purpose of each technique. Corresponding with each technique are tips on how to convey the technique and specific verbal examples of effective phrasing.

Technique	Purpose	How to Do This	Examples
Inviting	• Provides an opportunity for others to talk	• Signal you are interested in listening	"I'd like to hear about your problem."
Encouraging	• Conveys interest • Encourages speaker to elaborate	• Stay neutral • Mirror facial expressions • Nod head	"I see." "Uh-huh." "I'm listening."
Clarifying	• Confirms/refutes information already received	• Ask questions • Restate speaker's interpretation	"Is this what you mean?" "Please explain what you mean by 'aggressive behavior.'"
Paraphrasing	• Demonstrates that the listener understands what is being said	• Restate basic ideas and facts	"It sounds as if..." "So it seems you want..."
Reflecting	• Demonstrates that you understand how the person feels • Helps the person evaluate feelings	• Mirror the speaker's feelings	"You seem very upset."
Summarizing	• Reviews progress • Pulls together important ideas and facts • Establishes a basis for further discussion	• Restate major ideas expressed during the conversation	"These seem to be the key ideas you expressed."
Validating	• Acknowledges importance of other person	• Demonstrate appreciation for their efforts and actions	"I appreciate your willingness to resolve this problem."

FIGURE 8.7

Responsive Listening Techniques

STEPS TO MANAGE CONFLICT

Despite your best intentions, there may be times when a lack of communication results in conflict between you and your paraprofessional. It is during these uncomfortable situations that you feel at a loss of how to address the problem without arousing defensiveness or eroding self-esteem. Being aware of basic conflict management strategies in advance of a problem will relieve some of the anxieties associated with these stressful situations. Steps in conflict management include identifying the issue, determining the choices for a solution, planning a conference, and implementing a plan (Covey, 1989).

IDENTIFICATION OF THE ISSUE

When immersed in conflict with your paraprofessional, you should first identify and clarify the issue. Trying to be as objective as possible in determining the role that you have played in the misunderstanding is perhaps one of the most difficult reflections that you will need to make. Questions that will help you in this reflection are:

How are my attitudes, assumptions, and judgments affecting this situation?"

"Can I change my reactions?"

"Does the problem affect the learning, well-being, or

safety of the students?"

DETERMINATION OF POSSIBLE SOLUTIONS

Once you have clarified the problem and the role that you may play in the conflict, a tentative list of solutions can be generated. This list includes strategies that you can use to address the conflict.

SCHEDULE A CONFERENCE

An opportunity to discuss the issue should be scheduled at a time that is mutually agreeable for both you and your paraprofessional. In order to provide full attention to the issue, we suggest that the conference be held in a private, quiet location away from interruptions and outside distractions. Rehearsing what will be said during the conference will help you to use clear, nonjudgmental language such as:

"I am concerned when the children are left unsupervised."

"I can't start reading groups until you're here. Is there

something that is preventing you from arriving on time?"

DEVELOPMENT OF A COLLABORATIVE PLAN OF ACTION

During the conference between you and your paraprofessional, a plan of action should be developed. This plan includes a clear description of what the problem is, a list of possible solutions to the problem, a prioritization of the most effective solutions to the problem, and a description of who is responsible for implementing the solution (see Figure 8.8).

If the problem persists, you and your paraprofessional need to schedule another meeting. Possible revisions to the solution may need to occur, or the next prioritized solution on the plan needs to be discussed and implemented. Figure 8.9 asks you to reflect on your working environment.

EVALUATION OF THE TEACHER/PARAPROFESSIONAL TEAM PROCESS

Researchers have found that scheduling regular daily or weekly meetings between teachers and their paraprofessionals is crucial to maintaining open lines of communication (Wallace et al., 2001). Keeping a running agenda of issues and action plans helps to clarify student issues and establish accountability and consistency among teachers and paraprofessionals in addressing these concerns. Figure 8.10 provides a sample agenda format.

In order to adjust to the evolving needs of the instructional team, we recommend a periodic evaluation of your teacher/paraprofessional team process several times throughout the school year. A checklist has been provided to help you and your paraprofessional through this reflective process (Figure 8.11). Figure 8.12 asks you to reflect on the instructional team.

FIGURE 8.8

Collaborative Action
Plan

Date	
Members	
Perceived problem	
Possible solutions	1. 2. 3. 4.
Identify solution and person responsible	
Follow-up meeting date	

FIGURE 8.9

Take a Moment

Think About	Reflect	Respond
The working environment	What kind of working environment exists between you and your paraprofessional? How can you assess the needs of your paraprofessional? How will this improve your working environment? How can you and your paraprofessional work together to foster open communication?	

FIGURE 8.10

Sample Agenda
Format

Issue	Action	Who	When	Effective Response (complete at follow-up meeting)

FIGURE 8.11

Instructional Team
Checklist

Teachers should use this checklist periodically to examine the strengths and needs of the instructional team.	Yes	No

1. We hold consistent, regularly scheduled meetings.

2. Our meetings are student centered and are guided by a systematic agenda that includes issues of concern, how the issue will be addressed, who is responsible for the action, timeline for the action, and follow-up on the action.

3. We are clear on our job roles and responsibilities. The paraprofessional understands the county or district criteria by which he or she will be evaluated.

4. The paraprofessional's strengths and areas of need have been assessed and instructional responsibilities and trainings have been implemented accordingly.

5. The instructional team is aware of the goals and objectives for the students, how the goals and objections are being addressed through the curriculum, the progress each student is making, and expectations for future growth.

6. Feedback from the students has assessed the effectiveness of the instructional team and this information has been shared openly and constructively.

FIGURE 8.12

Take a Moment

Think About	Reflect	Respond
Evaluation of the instructional team	How do you evaluate the teacher/paraprofessional team process in your classroom? What evidence do you use?	

WORKING WITH NOVICE AND EXPERIENCED PARAPROFESSIONALS

Novice and experienced paraprofessionals both bring individual strengths and challenges to your professional partnership. In order to capitalize on the individual strengths of your paraprofessionals it is important to understand the unique perspectives both novice and experienced paraprofessionals bring to the classroom. Figure 8.13 generalizes the benefits and challenges of working with inexperienced and experienced paraprofessionals.

Developing an effective partnership with novice and/or experienced paraprofessionals may require different interaction and communication strategies. If you are working with both a novice and an experienced paraprofessional, you may often find yourself switching between a number of techniques and strategies that match their unique needs. Figure 8.14 provides you with a quick overview of strategies that meet the individual needs of novice and experienced paraprofessionals. Figure 8.15 and Figure 8.16 provide further clarification of the communication strategies listed in Figure 8.14.

INSTRUCTING ENGLISH LANGUAGE LEARNERS

As a special education teacher, you are continuously adapting and modifying your instruction and curriculum to make subject-matter content accessible to your students. When students with special needs come to you as English language learners (ELLs), you are responsible for identifying and implementing strategies that not only address their strengths and disabilities but also their linguistic diversity. IEPs for ELL students with special needs must include language needs as well as those for identified disabilities.

Because of the limited number of qualified bilingual teachers, many schools use bilingual aides or paraprofessionals to provide instruction to ELL students with special needs. Although using paraprofessionals in this role can be effective, it is important to remember that you should provide the majority of instruction. Taking the primary role

FIGURE 8.13

Benefits and Challenges of Working with Novice and Experienced Paraprofessionals

Working with Novice Paraprofessionals

Benefits	Challenges
Blank slates: come to you with little or no preconceived ideas of how to manage or instruct students.	Blank slates: May need extensive training in all aspects of instruction, classroom management, paperwork, class schedules, and interacting with colleagues and parents.
As the new person in the classroom, they typically are less resistant to redirection or constructive criticism.	Need clear and immediate feedback on their performance.
Open to new ideas and strategies. Enthusiastic to try new things.	They may not know what they don't know! Don't assume they know the basics. Give them clear and concise directions for tasks and expectations of their instruction and interactions with students.

FIGURE 8.13   Working with Experienced Paraprofessionals
(continued)

Benefits	Challenges
May have a good understanding of school bureaucracy and can help you navigate through logistics and paperwork (e.g., bus schedules, lunch count, attendance sheets).	May have difficulty in discriminating between their role as paraprofessional and your role as teacher. May generalize their expertise in working within the school culture to being the teacher in charge of the classroom.
May have a historical record of successful instructional and behavioral strategies used in the classroom. This information may guide your selection and implementation of present strategies.	Past experience may influence willingness to try new strategies or revise strategies used by a previous instructor. May be resistant to change and will compare you to the previous teacher, (e.g.,"Mr. Smith never let the kids do that!").
May be well connected to the community. These community connections can lead to better connections with parents and can guide you to resources for your classroom.	Living in the same community for an extended period of time may lead to close friendships and may potentially result in "gossiping" and breaching professional confidentiality with students and parents.
May offer you insights and connections into the cultural and societal norms of your school community.	Role as a paraprofessional may conflict with cultural norms of status in their cultural grouping. For example, asking your paraprofessional to intercede in an issue with a parent may be in conflict with directly contacting the elder of the cultural group.

in the education of your English language learners will help to refute the premise that bilingual education is remedial education and will keep you connected to the needs of all your students (Baca & Cervantes, 2004).

As the teacher of record, it is your responsibility to provide training for your paraprofessionals not only in modification and adaptations for the students' special needs, but also in basic instructional strategies for English language learners. You will find that many of the strategies that you use for making curriculum accessible for your students with special needs may also benefit your ELL students.

ELL STRATEGIES AND APPROACHES TO SHARE WITH YOUR PARAPROFESSIONAL

Research on English language learner with disabilities indicates that the following instructional activities promote the most intensive and sustainable levels of engaged learning (Baca & Cervantes, 2004):

■ Tap into students' prior knowledge and encourage them to share their life experiences.

Strategies for
Working
Effectively with
Paraprofessionals

Strategy	N	E
Conduct a needs assessment of their perceived strengths and needs.	X	X
Review and clarify district/county evaluation form and evaluation procedures.	X	X
Provide clear expectations of their role as a paraprofessional in your classroom.	X	X
Use as a resource for school and community resources.		X
Seek out assistance with school schedules and routines.		X
Provide clear and reasonably immediate feedback on their performance (constructive and positive).	X	X
"Clear the air" when a problem or issue arises. Don't assume it will go away if you ignore it. (See Figure 8.15.)	X	X
Examine possible reasons for resistance. Explore solutions. Use indirect language. (See Figure 8.16.)		X
Provide on-going formal and informal training.	X	X
Convey appreciation and respect for their contributions.	X	X
Share in "mundane" or repetitive tasks.	X	X
Schedule consistent meeting times and reassess needs.	X	X
If issues continue, document your concerns and actions and discuss with your administrator.	X	X

N = (novice)   E = (experienced)

Clearing the Air

"I noticed that _____."

"I'm concerned that you may be (tired, sick, bored, etc)."

"Is this correct?"

"I am concerned because..."

"Do you need my assistance in addressing this concern?"

- Supplement abstract concepts with visual aids, manipulatives, and examples from students' previous experiences.
- Support the use of their native language.
- Encourage students who have difficulty in writing to tape-record answers in either the first or second language. Provide books and materials in their native language.

FIGURE 8.16
Resistance

Using Indirect Language

- May

- Might

- Perhaps

- Maybe

- It could be that...

Disagreeing in an Agreeable Way

"I understand what you're saying—we might also want to consider..."

"I see your point, and ..."

"Your point is important, and another interpretation (idea) might be..."

"That's an interesting point of view, and another way to look at it might be..."

"You may wish to consider..."

"I hear you, this is what I'm thinking..."

- Teach in context and stay away from isolated, decontextualized segments of information (rote learning or isolated drilling).
- Teach literacy through language-experience stories, dialogue journals, shared book experiences, and creative writing. Teach behavioral expectations through role playing and modeling.
- Build intrinsic motivation and feelings of accomplishment. Gradually increase the difficulty level as mastery of easier levels is achieved.
- Utilize peer collaboration.
- Match a student who has mastered a skill with another student needing assistance. This is most effective when the peer tutor is bilingual in both English and the native language of the student being tutored.

It merits repeating that you are responsible for the instruction of your students with EL special needs. Once your paraprofessional is trained in the previously listed strategies, it is imperative that you determine which strategies the paraprofessional is to use with individual students, that you continue to be the students' primary instructor, that you continuously monitor student progress, and that you make ongoing curriculum and instructional adaptations and modifications.

PARAPROFESSIONAL PERCEPTIONS

Low expectations of student performance and negative perceptions of their character have a direct effect on the quality of education students receive and can greatly factor into differences in student achievement (Brophy & Good, 1986; Good & Brophy, 1973; Rist, 1970).

Cultural stereotypes and lack of exposure to diversity can influence a paraprofessional's perceptions of students and their families. This lack of understanding can ultimately impact how they interact with students and how effective they are in their instruction. Often, differences in students' life experiences are interpreted as deficiencies in their environment. As teacher, it is important that you clarify that although some EL students may have different experiences than other students, they bring a wealth of experiences and skills into the classroom.

Positive perceptions and high expectations of students have proven to result in higher-quality educational opportunities. Monitoring paraprofessionals' verbal and non-verbal messages when working with EL students will help to ensure that the students are receiving positive messages regarding their abilities and contributions to the classroom.

CONCLUSION

As you reflect on the information provided in this chapter, it is important to remember that every special education teacher/paraprofessional working relationship is unique and is shaped by a variety of variables that may range from age, gender, culture, education, and family differences to learning and communication style preferences. Given this complexity, it is necessary for you to closely evaluate the overt and subtle environmental and interpersonal forces that determine the effectiveness of an instructional team. Experiencing the power of working together as a team dedicated to improving your students' social, emotional, and academic lives can be one of the most satisfying aspects of teaching.

EXPLORATIONS

1. Complete an individual preferences assessment such as the one shown in Figure 8.3. Ask your paraprofessional to read and complete an assessment also. Together, discuss how the similarities and differences in preferences may be addressed as you work together as a team in the classroom. What did you learn from this activity?
2. Develop a description or list of activities for paraprofessional training based on the results of your paraprofessional's responses to the paraprofessional needs assessment (Figure 8.4). Discuss your ideas for training with your paraprofessional. What does your paraprofessional think about your ideas? Does your paraprofessional have any suggestions for enhancing the training?
3. Review the responsive listening techniques chart in Figure 8.7. Identify which of the techniques you typically use the most. Which techniques do you typically use the least? Select one technique to focus on for one week and be mindful when you are using it. What are the outcomes when you are using this technique?

WEBSITES

National Resource Center for Paraprofessionals
http://www.nrcpara.org
This site provides links, articles, and a bibliography on training and managing paraprofessionals.

Paraprofessionals—FAQ
http://www.ericdigests.org/2000-4/factors.htm
This site lists the factors that influence the performance, development, and supervision of paraprofessionals.

Roles for Education Paraprofessionals in Effective Schools
http://ed.gov/pubs/Paraprofessionals/-index.html
This site provides listings of elements of good professional practice, clear definitions of roles and responsibilities of paraprofessionals, ongoing professional development, and profiles of effective programs.

REFERENCES

Baca, L., & Cervantes, H. (2004). *The bilingual special education interface* (4th ed.). Columbus, OH: Merrill/Prentice Hall.

Brophy, J., & Good, T. (1986). Teacher behavior and student achievement. In M. C. Wittrock (Ed.), *Handbook of research on teaching* (3rd ed., pp. 328–375). New York: Macmillian.

Bureau of Labor Statistics, U.S. Department of Labor. (2005). *Occupational outlook handbook.* Retrieved April 25, 2005 from *http://www.bls.gov/oco/ocos153.htm*

Causton-Theoharis, J. N., & Malmgren, K. W. (2005). Building bridges: Strategies to help paraprofessionals promote peer interaction. *Teaching Exceptional Children, 37*(6), 18–24.

Covey, S. R. (1989). *The seven habits of highly effective people.* New York: Simon and Schuster.

Crutchfield, M. (1997). Who's teaching our children with disabilities? *NICHY: National Clearinghouse for Professions in Special Education, 27*(8), 1–23.

Eagan, G. (1982). *The skilled helper: A model for systematic helping and interpersonal relating.* Monterey, CA: Brookes/Cole.

Gaylord, V., Wallace, T., Pickett, A. & Litkins, M. (2002). *Impact: Feature Issue on Paraeducators Supporting Students with Disabilities and At-Risk, 15*(2) [online]. Minneapolis: University of Minnesota, Institute on Community Integration. Retrieved April 25, 2005 from *http://ici.umn.edu/products/impact/152.*

Giangreco, M. F., & Broer, S. M. (2005). Questionable utilization of paraprofessionals in inclusive schools: Are we addressing the symptoms or causes? *Focus on Autism and Other Developmental Disabilities, 20*(1), 10–26.

Good, T. L., & Brophy, J. E. (1973). *Looking into classrooms.* New York: Harper & Row.

Norwood, G. (1996). Maslow's hierarchy of needs. Retrieved April 25, 2005 from *http://www.connect.net/georgen/maslow.htm.*

Pickett, A. (2002). Paraeducators: The evolution in their roles, responsibilities, training, and supervision. Retrieved April 25, 2005 from *http://ici.umn.edu/products/impact/152/over2.html.*

Rist, R. (1970). Student social class and leader expectations: The self-fulling prophecy in ghetto education. *Harvard Eduucational Review, 40,* 411–451.

Twachtman-Cullen, D. (1998). *How to be a para pro: A comprehensive training manual for paraprofessionals.* Connecticut: Starfish Specialty Press.

Wallace, T., Shin, J., Bartholomay, T., & Stahl, B. (2001). Knowledge and skills for teachers supervising the work of paraprofessionals. *Exceptional Children, 67*(4), 520–533.

9

Collaborative Consultation

"A goal without a plan is just a wish."

Antoine de Saint-Exupery

CHAPTER OBJECTIVES

- Describe collaborative consultation
- Explain the benefits/challenges of collaborative consultation
- Provide strategies for addressing resistance
- Describe collaborative consultation steps
- Discuss professional ethics

Before reading this chapter, consider your past experiences with school consultation. Were you an active participant in the decision-making process? Did engaging in consultation positively impact the teachers you work with and your students? What were some of the challenges you faced when consulting with your colleagues? Record your reflections and revisit your response as you read this chapter.

INTRODUCTION

Collaborative consultation is an essential element in providing appropriate services to an increasingly diverse and complex student population (Dettmer, Thurston, & Dyck, 2005). This chapter introduces you to a process of collaborative consultation and provides several strategies for working successfully with other professionals within your school setting.

The focus of this chapter is to provide practical information and organizational tools that will streamline your collaboration efforts. We encourage you to begin collaborating with other teachers on your school campus before any problems occur. However, a major role performed by special education teachers is to provide consultation to other teachers at the school site in regard to students' behavior and learning abilities. Typically, this consultation process takes place between you, the special educator, as the consultant, and a general education teacher as the consultee. To help you facilitate this process, we offer a research-based collaborative model with accompanying interview protocols and problem-solving worksheets. We believe that the benefit of this approach is that it requires both teachers to work together to create a viable method to address a student's behavior problem or learning difficulty. Practicing the strategies in this chapter fosters the relationship between general education and special education teachers to promote the academic and social growth of all students.

DESCRIPTION OF COLLABORATIVE CONSULTATION

Collaborative consultation is a systematic process that promotes interaction among a variety of school personnel and results in the creation and implementation of educational plans that are in the best academic and social interest of students. Key players in collaborative consultation include:

- *Consultee:* The person who seeks educational assistance for a student.
- *Consultant:* The person whom the consultee requests to provide professional advice or services in a field of special knowledge and training.
- *Client:* The student who benefits directly from the collaboration between the consultant and consultee.

WHAT A COLLABORATIVE CONSULTATION LOOKS LIKE

When you engage in collaborative consultation you may participate in several of the following activities:

- Actively listen to colleagues' ideas and concerns.
- Schedule times to confer with colleagues and plan observations as needed.
- Collect data to confirm colleagues' concerns.
- Provide instructional accommodations for students.
- Share methods for data collection.
- Provide assistive technology support.
- Model effective instructional and behavioral strategies.
- Gather information and resources for your colleagues.
- Connect your colleagues with professionals and agencies.
- Plan and co-teach a lesson with your colleague.

WHAT A COLLABORATIVE CONSULTATION DOES NOT LOOK LIKE

As a special educator, it is important to understand the parameters of the role you play as a collaborative consultant and to not assume inappropriate roles and responsibilities. A collaborative school consultant is not a:

- Licensed therapist or counselor. Consultation should revolve around student issues, not the individual problems of your colleague (West & Idol, 1987).
- Private school consultant. When done collaboratively, all members of the consultative team assume equal responsibility and accountability for the student's progress.

BENEFITS/CHALLENGES OF COLLABORATIVE CONSULTATION

BENEFITS

Implementing the collaborative consultation model can result in many benefits for students, teachers, and schools (Idol, Nevin, Paolucci-Whitcomb, 2000). Direct benefits for students with exceptionalities include:

- Receiving planned instruction for academic and behavioral problems in the least restrictive environment

- Minimizing labeling and social isolation
- Establishing continuity between their general and special education programs
- Minimizing confusion over IEP goals and objectives
- Receiving instructional services that are based on academic and social needs

All learners benefit from instruction when teachers share varying areas of expertise and resources.

Indirect benefits for students are (Dettmer et al., 2005; Idol et al., 2000):

- Changing colleagues' belief systems regarding the education of learners with exceptionalities
- Alleviating stress that is often a product of teacher isolation
- Increasing general and special educators' knowledge of curriculum, instruction, and classroom management

CHALLENGES

Collaborative consultation requires multiple interactions between educators from a variety of disciplines. This collaborative process requires effective communication and organizational skills (Friend & Cook, 2003; Kampwirth, 2003). Some of these challenges have been identified as:

- *Planning and time management:* Teachers struggle to balance the time they spend planning and implementing instruction with scheduling and conducting collaborative meetings.
- *Scheduling meetings:* Scheduling collaborative meetings can be challenging when team members are on different time schedules and/or have additional responsibilities outside the classroom.
- *Enhancing interpersonal relationships:* Misunderstandings and confusion can occur if team members don't share common goals for the student. Teachers may have different teaching styles and philosophies and may be uncomfortable having another teacher enter their classroom.

Figure 9.1 provides you with strategies for dealing with possible roadblocks to the collaborative consultation process.

ISSUES RELATED TO RESISTANCE

There may come a time when your most well-planned collaborative efforts are met with resistance. This resistance may be generated from a variety of sources, including your interactions with parents, colleagues, paraprofessionals, and/or administrators. It is important to understand that although resistance is typically considered to be a negative response during collaboration, it often is a necessary step during the process of change. The following section will explore why people are resistant, describe the indicators of resistance, and provide you with ways that you can effectively manage resistance and negativity.

UNDERSTANDING RESISTANCE

Resistance is a common response when people are asked to change their thoughts, actions, and/or belief systems (Dettmer et al., 2005). Resistance often has little correlation

FIGURE 9.1

Addressing
Challenges of
Collaborative
Consultation

Source: From Peggy
Dettmer et al. *Consulta-
tion, collaboration, and
teamwork for students
with special needs,* 5e.
Published by Allyn and
Bacon, Boston, MA.
Copyright © 2005 by
Pearson Education.
Reprinted by permission
of the publisher.

Planning and Time Management

- Time management is primarily about choices. Analyze your current use of time and establish goals and priorities for consultation.
- Use a daily/weekly planner to help you keep track of multiple responsibilities.
- Take large tasks and break them into smaller activities that you can successfully achieve in a reasonable amount of time.
- Assign a due date for every responsibility involved in the consultation process.
- Delegate routine tasks to students, paraprofessionals, or parent volunteers when possible. This will free your time for planning and consulting.
- Schedule your most difficult tasks during the time of the day you are feeling most energized.
- Learn to say "no" to those tasks that fall outside of your primary goals.
- Create a well-organized area to work. Avoid the "stacked desk syndrome" (MacKenzie & Waldo, 1981), where you are unable to find important documents due to clutter.

Scheduling Meetings

- Schedule meetings during joint prep times and lunch hours.
- Explore the possibility of meeting before or after regularly scheduled meetings (such as faculty or grade-level meetings).
- Some schools are given one release day per week for collaborative activities. This time is balanced by slightly increasing the instructional hours of four out of the five workdays.

Enhancing Interpersonal Relationships

Stop: Avoid judging and taking on the role of expert.

Look: Picking up on your consultee's signals of discomfort or resistance will help you address the issue with clarity at the front end of problem solving.

Listen: Listening attentively to your consultee conveys a message of respect for his or her ideas and professional integrity.

to the new idea being presented or the expertise of the person who is trying to implement the change. People may resist change for the following reasons:

- They are comfortable with the status quo; it is nonthreatening.
- They feel that change would have undesirable results for them and/or for their students/child/family.
- They are uncertain as to what effect the change would have on them and/or their students/child/family.
- They are uncertain whether they have the expertise to implement the change.
- They feel overwhelmed with other responsibilities.
- They have alternate philosophies, values, or beliefs.
- They have alternate cultural perceptions.
- They perceive there is poor planning or design for implementation of change.

HOW TO DETECT RESISTANCE

Dettmer et al. (2005) estimate that as much as 80% of problem solving requires working through some form of resistance. Friend and Cook (2003, p. 26) list the following indicators and examples of resistance:

- Refusing to participate on any level: "I just can't deal with doing that right now."

- Verbally supporting change, but failing to follow through in actions: "Sure, that's great."
- Displacing responsibility to another person: "The parents aren't going to like this."
- Deferring change to a time in the future: "This is a bad time of year to make changes."
- Relying on status quo practices: "We've always done it this way."

MANAGING RESISTANCE

The first step in dealing with resistance is to come to terms with your own feelings of defensiveness. It is important to remember that the underlying reasons for resistance are most often not of a personal nature but are purely an emotional response. If you respond emotionally to resistance by becoming defensive or angry, your colleague will respond in kind. This "push and pull" cycle is not only emotionally exhausting but often results in damaging any present or future collaborative relationships. When faced with resistance, there are three possible outcomes according to Gordon (1977):

I Win—You Lose

or

You Win—I Lose

or

I Win—You Win

The first two outcomes are indicative of the unproductive "push and pull" cycle mentioned previously. Covey (1989), believing that the "I win—you win" outcome preserves relationships and fosters effective collaboration, lists four steps in the "win-win" approach:

1. Use empathic listening to gain an understanding of the other person's point of view. Listening with empathy and concern is fundamental to this four-step process. Listening openly without judgment to someone who is resistant or upset will help you focus on the problem, not the emotion. Empathic listening also provides the resistant or angry person with time to gain composure and lowers his or her emotional affect so he or she is more receptive to feedback. It is almost impossible to argue or disagree with someone who will not argue or disagree back. Uninterrupted, empathetic listening will help dissipate anger and will break the spiral of resistance.

2. Identify key issues of concern. After listening carefully to the other person's viewpoint, you will need to summarize the main points of concern and verify whether you are stating his or her concerns accurately. You will need to listen to the person's feedback carefully and readjust your understanding of the issues as appropriate. Verification of the other person's concerns is the pivotal step that leads to formation of acceptable solutions.

3. Jointly create a list of acceptable solutions. This process needs to take place with the understanding that all suggested solutions are to be considered without predisposed judgments. Using language that is permissive and indirect may aid you in arriving at solutions that are mutually acceptable.

4. Search for creative ways to meet your goal. Collective problem solving will greatly enhance your ability to come up with an effective solution. Jointly developing action steps for addressing concerns ensures ownership of solutions and underscores feelings of respect.

COMMON STEPS IN THE CONSULTATION PROCESS

Various models of the consultation process have been developed and researched over the last 30 years. The model presented in this guidebook is comprised of seven steps and represents a flexible, collaborative, problem-solving approach that addresses the changing needs of students and teachers (Gutkin & Curtis, 1990).

STEP ONE: IDENTIFY AND CLARIFY THE PROBLEM

Identifying the student's problem behavior or learning difficulty is the most critical step in the consultation process. The lack of a clear and unbiased analysis of the problem may result in the consultant and consultee spending valuable time and effort on the wrong problem or two entirely different problems. Use of verbal prompts such as:

- Can you expand on that thought?
- Can you recall what happened when . . .?
- Are you saying that . . .?
- What did you mean when you said that . . .?
- Can you tell me a little more about . . .?

in combination with a problem identification process will assist you in clarifying important issues surrounding the concern and will ultimately result in the determination of appropriate interventions. Figure 9.2 will help to guide you through this process.

STEP TWO: ANALYZE THE ORIGIN OF THE PROBLEM

Student behavior and learning may be affected by a variety of influences inside and outside of the classroom environment. As a consultant, you need to gather information about the student's current academic testing, health and attendance records, social and emotional well-being, and issues of diversity that may be contributing to the problem.

STEP THREE: DISCUSS ALTERNATIVE STRATEGIES

Once the problem has been clearly identified, you should meet with your consultee to discuss possible strategies to address the concern. These strategies should be generated collaboratively and should represent a collection of ideas that are both creative and practical. Figure 9.3 provides you with a process for generating these strategies.

STEP FOUR: PRIORITIZE AND SELECT A STRATEGY

Once you generate a list of strategies in step three, you will need to guide your consultee through a process of determining which strategy will be most effective and practical to implement. Guiding a discussion that requires your consultee to numerically prioritize the strategies from most effective to least effective will assist your consultee in choosing a strategy that will be practical to implement. It is imperative for your consultee to have the ultimate say in determining which of the strategies discussed in step three will be implemented in the classroom. This "buy-in" will help circumvent your consultee's resistance to trying the new strategy and will give the consultee equal accountability in the success or failure of the plan. Figure 9.3 provides a means to document the priority decided upon for each strategy.

FIGURE 9.2

Problem
Identification
Interview Protocol

Consultant _____ Teacher _____ Date ___/___/___ School _____

Student Information:

Name _____

Room _____ Grade _____ Age _____ Sex: M   F   IEP: Y   N

Describe the problem behavior or learning difficulty. (5 minutes)

Consultee prepare ahead Verification by consultant	

Describe other items that seem to be related to the problem behavior or learning difficulty. (3 minutes)

Consultee prepare ahead Verification by consultant	

Describe the conditions under which the problem behavior or learning difficulty is most likely to occur. (2 minutes)

Consultee prepare ahead

When:

_____

Where:

_____

With Whom:

_____

(continued)

FIGURE 9.2

(continued)

Describe what usually happens after the problem behavior or learning difficulty occurs. (2 minutes)	
Consultee prepare ahead Verification by consultant	

Describe what usually happens immediately before the problem behavior or learning difficulty occurs. (2 minutes)	
Consultee prepare ahead Verification by consultant	

Describe what you usually do when the problem behavior or learning difficulty occurs. (2 minutes)	
Consultee prepare ahead Verification by consultant	

If applicable, describe what other students do when the problem behavior or learning difficulty occurs. (2 minutes)	
Consultee prepare ahead Verification by consultant	

Describe what you would like the student to do instead of the problem behavior, or what evidence is needed to demonstrate that the student has overcome his or her learning difficulty. (2 minutes)	
Consultee prepare ahead Verification by consultant	
List or describe other interventions that have been tried. (3 minutes)	
Consultee prepare ahead Verification by consultant	
Make an appointment to conduct an observation and debriefing. (1 minute) Date ____/____/____ Time ____: ____; to ____: ____ Place/Classroom _____ Other information/notes Consultant	
Assessment data needed Instruments to be used	

STEP FIVE: DETERMINE RESPONSIBILITIES

Successful implementation of the strategy chosen in step four involves careful planning as to the "who, what, where, how, and when" of the plan. Implementation steps are also recorded on the form shown in Figure 9.3. Determining specific roles and responsibilities and accountability for timelines is crucial to maintaining a positive collaborative partnership.

FIGURE 9.3

Problem-Solving Worksheet

Source: From Peggy Dettmer et al. *Consultation, collaboration, and teamwork for students with special needs,* 5e. Published by Allyn and Bacon, Boston, MA. Copyright © 2005 by Pearson Education. Reprinted by permission of the publisher.

Consultee: _____

Consultant: _____

Date: _____

Problem:

Options	Possible Consequences	Priority
1.		
2.		
3.		
4.		

Chosen solution: #_____

Implementation Steps	Who	When

How will you assess the effectiveness of your solution?

STEP SIX: IMPLEMENT THE STRATEGY

During this step, it is critical that you meet regularly with your consultee. Kampwirth (2003) posits that implementing the new strategy may result in a series of additional issues:

- The focus of the problem shifts.
- The consultee needs additional resources to implement the strategy.
- The consultee feels unprepared or untrained to use the new strategy with the student.
- The student reacts to the new strategy in an unexpected way or the rest of the class is affected negatively by the intervention.

If any of these issues surface, it is vital for you to immediately meet with your consultee and revisit steps three through five. Choosing the second prioritized strategy listed in step four may be helpful if the focus of the concern remains the same.

STEP SEVEN: ASSESS THE EFFECTIVENESS OF THE STRATEGY

Following steps one through seven will result in one of several possible outcomes, according to Kampwirth (2003):

- The strategy chosen will address the issue of concern.

FIGURE 9.4

Checklist for
Evaluating
Collaborative
Consultation

Source: From Peggy.
Dettmer et al. *Consulta-
tion, collaboration, and
teamwork for students
with special needs,* 5e.
Published by Allyn and
Bacon, Baston, MA.
Copyright © 2005 by
Pearson Education.
Reprinted by permission
of the publisher.

Consultant I worked with: _____

Consultee filling out this form: _____

My consultant:

	A Strength	OK	Needs Improvement
1. Demonstrated flexibility			
2. Communicated Clearly			
3. Used our time productively			
4. Listened to my concerns			
5. Provided me with information and resources			
6. Respected my experience and knowledge			
7. Continued to monitor my students' progress and achievement			

8. I plan to continue seeking opportunities to consult with the consultant again.
   Yes _____ No_____

Other comments:

- ■ The strategy chosen will have some positive results but will need additional modifications.
- ■ The strategy chosen will have minimal success and will require a complete recycling through the steps.

In order to continue to develop your skills as a consultant, it is important that you assess the effectiveness of the consultative process with your collaborative partner and make adjustments as needed. Figure 9.4 provides a quick and easy way for you to get feedback from your partner in regard to your collaborative consultation skills.

PROFESSIONAL ETHICS

Collaborative consultation requires knowledge, flexibility, effective communication skills, and the ability to be adaptable and resilient. The collaborative aspects of consultation also require an awareness of the ethical issues surrounding such interactions. As a consultant you will need to adhere to the following ethical practices (Brown, Pryzwansky, & Schulte, 2001; Friend & Cook, 2003):

1. *Competence:* You need to possess the knowledge and skills necessary for addressing the issue of concern. You should take active steps to maintain and increase your level of expertise through professional development activities. If you don't feel competent, it is your responsibility to assist the consultee in finding the necessary specialist or resources to address the concern.

FIGURE 9.5

Take a Moment

Think About	Reflect	Respond
Past experiences as a consultation team member	What role did you play as the consultant in the decision-making process?	
	What role did you play as the consultee in the decision-making process?	
	What impact did your consultative efforts have on your student's academic/behavioral progress?	
	What challenges did you experience when you were engaging in consultation?	

2. *Protecting the welfare of the student:* The well-being of the student needs to remain the focus of the consultation. Development and implementation of interventions should be based on solid research practice.

3. *Maintaining confidentiality:* Preservation of confidentiality must be maintained by both the consultant and the consultee. This applies to issues of confidentiality concerning not only the client and his or her family, but also to the consultee and other school employees.

4. *Social and moral responsibility:* As a consultant your actions must be governed by the best interest of the student. Be careful not to let religious, political, or cultural biases dictate your decisions. Imposing your own values into the decision-making process is unethical and unprofessional.

5. *Belief in parity:* This principle is based on the belief that the student will benefit most fully from an eclectic approach to consultation. All members of the consultative team should command equal respect and importance. This principle provides the framework for the model of collaborative consultation.

Figure 9.5 asks you to reflect on past experiences as a consultation team member.

CONCLUSION

Collaborative consultation is a challenging but effective method for addressing the needs of children with exceptionalities (Friend & Cook, 2003; Kampwirth, 2003). This method is effective only when all parties are actively engaged and are working toward the same goal. As a consultant you must avoid the role of the "sole expert" and work toward establishing a partnership that is based on parity, trust, and ethical practices. When practiced with clarity, this method will not only benefit all learners but will also enhance your knowledge, skills, and long-term relationships with your colleagues—a win-win situation for all!

EXPLORATIONS

1. List four to five major professional and recreational interests you enjoy. Infusion of these interests in casual conversations with your colleagues will build rapport for future consultations.
2. What specific barriers to collaborative consultation do you encounter in your role as a special educator? Based on the information in this chapter, list ways you plan to address these barriers.
3. Meet with your administrator to learn more about his or her perceptions of the benefits of collaborative consultation. Explore systemic changes that could be made to support the process of multiple collaborative meetings.
4. How will practicing collaborative consultation benefit: (a) your students with exceptionalities, (b) the students in general education classrooms, (c) your professional development, and (d) your consultee's professional development?
5. Ethical considerations must guide all consultations and collaborative efforts. Make a list of the guiding principles that define your role as a special educator. How do your principles differ from or support the ethical issues of consultation discussed in this chapter?

WEBSITES

Center for Applied Specialized Technology (CAST): General and Special Education Associations
http://www.cast.org/publications/ncac/ncac/gened.html
This site has information on general and special education collaboration for accessing the general education curriculum.

Collaboration Between General and Special Education Teacher ERIC Digest: ED 409317
http://www.ericdigests.org/1998-1/general.htm
This site provides full-text access to ERIC access to ERIC Digest 409317 on general and special education teacher collaboration.

Collaborative Teaching: Special Education for Inclusive Classrooms
http://www/parrotpublishing.com
This site presents an online textbook that discusses topics of collaboration between general and special education teachers.

Council for Exceptional Children (CEC)
http://eriece.org/fag/regsped.html
This site links to ERIC digests, related Internet resources, and discussion groups on the topic of how general and special education teachers can work together efficiently.

General and Special Education Collaborative
http://www.iu08.org/gsec/
This site describes Pennsylvania's statewide effort to promote collaboration between general and special educators.

IDEA 04 and Research for Inclusive Settings (IRIS) Center
http://iris.peabody.vanderbilt.edu/browsebytopic03.html
This site offers resources, materials, and training modules on the topic of collaboration. No cost downloads are available.

Publication for the National Center on Secondary education and Transition
http://www.ncset.org/publications/viewdesc.asp?id=1097
This site provides creative and innovative strategies to promote collaboration between general and special education personnel.

REFERENCES

Brown, D., Pryzwansky, W. B., & Schulte, A. C. (2001). *Psychological consultation: Introduction to theory and practice.* Boston: Allyn & Bacon.

Dettmer, P., Thurston, L., & Dyck, N. (2005). *Consultation, collaboration, and teamwork for students with special needs.* Boston: Pearson Education Inc.

Friend, M., & Cook, L. (2003). *Interactions: Collaboration skills for school professionals.* Boston: Allyn & Bacon.

Gordon, T. (1997). *Leader effectiveness training.* New York: Wyden Books.

Gutkin, T. B., & Curtis, M. (1990). School-based consultation: Theory, techniques, and research. In C. R. Reynolds & T. B. Gutkin (Eds.), *The handbook of school psychology* (2nd ed., pp. 577–611). New York: Wiley.

Idol, L., Nevin A., & Paolucci-Whitcomb, P. (2000) *Collaborative consultation* (3rd ed.). Austin, TX: Pro-Ed.

Kampwirth, T. (2003). *Collaborative consultation in the schools: Effective practices for students with learning and behavior problems.* Upper Saddle River, NJ: Merrill/Prentice Hall.

MacKenzie, A., & Waldo, K. C. (1981). *About time! A woman's guide to time management.* New York: McGraw-Hill.

Thurston, L. (1987). *Survival skills for women: Facilitator manual.* Manhattan, KS: Survival Skills and Development.

West, J. F., & Idol, L. (1987). School consultation (Part I): An interdisciplinary perspective on theory, models, and research. *Journal of Learning Disabilities, 20*(7), 385–408.

10
Home–School Partnerships

"Families are big, small, extended, nuclear, multigenerational, with one parent, two parents, and grandparents. We live under one roof, or many. A family can be as temporary as a few weeks, or as permanent as forever. We become a part of a family by birth, adoption, marriage, or from a desire for mutual support. . . . A family is a culture unto itself, with different values and unique ways of realizing its dreams; together our families become a source of our rich cultural heritage. . . . Our families create neighborhoods, communities, states and nations."

Report on the House Memorial 5 Task Force on Young
Children and Families (1990, New Mexico)

CHAPTER OBJECTIVES

- ▥ Describe the legislative mandates and educational rationale for developing family partnerships
- ▥ Provide a basis for understanding families
- ▥ Describe the steps for collaborating with parents
- ▥ Discuss tips for parent–teacher conferencing
- ▥ Present strategies for including parents in decision making

> *Education of the whole student requires collaborative partnerships. In previous chapters we have discussed strategies for developing collaborative relationships with paraprofessionals and teachers. An essential collaborative component for the success of your students is your partnership with families. Before reading this chapter consider the following: Do you believe that family involvement benefits the education of your students? How much does your understanding of family constructs influence your ability to communicate effectively with parents? Record your reflections and revisit your response as you read this chapter.*

INTRODUCTION

Developing partnerships with families is one of the most critical and challenging aspects of your job as a special educator. As an educator, you work in highly diverse settings and interact with families from many different backgrounds.

Forming these partnerships not only requires the use of effective communications skills, but also requires an understanding of individual differences among families and self-evaluation of your own perceptions of diversity (Chen, McLean, Corso & Bruns, 2001; Turnbull, Rothstein-Fisch, Greenfield, & Quiroz, 2001). Gaining an understanding of and respect for your families' unique constructs will lead to improved communication and facilitate their mandated participation in decision-making meetings.

Legal Mandates and Educational Rationale for Developing Family Partnerships

As a special educator you should be aware of several current legislative mandates that dictate the development of home and school partnerships:

- Reauthorization of the Individuals with Disabilities Education Act (IDEA; 2004)—Clarifies and strengthens parental rights and involvement in all educational decision-making processes. This includes the participation of parents in newly formed community transition councils.
- No Child Left Behind (NCLB; 2002)—Includes requirements about parental involvement, highly qualified teachers, and researched-based instruction. NCLB mandates that schools must measure and report students' progress to parents.
- Goals 2000: Educate America Act—Focuses on parent involvement in promoting the academic, social, and emotional well-being of children.

Research supporting the connection between home–school partnerships and increased student development provides the rationale for building strong family partnerships and underscores legislative mandates (Christenson & Cleary, 1990; Hansen, Himes, & Meier, 1990). Families as well as students also benefit from this collaboration. Family members who are actively involved in their child's education report improved feelings of self-esteem and an increased connection with their community (Dettmer, Thurston, & Dyck, 2005).

Understanding Families

Developing an understanding of the unique issues facing parents of children with exceptionalities is essential in forging partnerships with families. The empathy you gain from examining the stages of grieving and family life cycles will help prepare you for dealing with the resistance and anger that sometimes accompanies interactions with families with children with exceptionalities. Additionally, appreciation for the cultural diversity found in families will help you to build stronger home–school partnerships.

The Grieving Process

As a special educator it is crucial that you begin to understand the emotional impact that accompanies the diagnosis of a student's disability. Knowledge that their child has a disability can often shatter parental dreams and produce deep feelings of loss and despair. Dr. Ken Moses (1987) proposes that supporting parents through the grieving process allows them to work through this loss and generate new dreams for their child.

Special educators need to understand that grieving is not a step-by-step process that evolves through discrete stages (Moses, 1987). For example, a parent of a 13-year-old adolescent may still experience the grieving state of denial when faced with the prospect of his or her child transitioning into high school. It is important to remember that the stages of grieving do not adhere to any rigid order and are as individual as the families who are experiencing them.

The following is a brief summary of Ken Moses's (1987) research on the stages of the grieving process:

- *Denial*. Denial can protect the family from the initial shock of the diagnosis or any new challenges that they may be confronting. It can be expressed by feelings of sadness, confusion, or helplessness. Special educators need to be sensitive to this response when they are relaying new or critical information regarding the student's disability. It is important not to overwhelm the parent with information during this stage of grieving.

- ▩ *Anxiety*. Families facing the overwhelming responsibility of doing what is best for their child's physical, emotional, and academic well-being often become anxious and agitated. Moses considers anxiety to being the catalyst for helping parents move forward in planning for their child's future.

- ▩ *Fear*. Significant loss can produce "a profound sense of abandonment and vulnerability" (Moses, 1987, p. 4). These feelings can result in a general sense of fear of what the future holds for the child and family members. Parents experiencing this stage often appear to be overprotective.

- ▩ *Guilt*. Parents generally express guilt in one of two ways: (1) assuming full responsibility for "causing" their child's disability, (2) believing that the disability is punishment for a past misdeed or thought. Guilt can allow parents to confront the loss and redefine the issue of cause and responsibility.

- ▩ *Depression*. This is a common response and should be viewed as a necessary feeling of the grieving process. This state is commonly expressed by sighing deeply or crying and allows parents to come to terms with what it means to be a competent and capable parent of a child with exceptionalities.

- ▩ *Anger*. This is the most disconcerting of the feeling states for families and teachers. As parents experience feelings of loss and despair, this anger may be projected onto family members, doctors, support-service providers, and teachers. Expressing anger "opens the way to address the meaning of justice" and "clears the way to getting on with the task at hand" (Moses, 1987, p. 7).

Figure 10.1 summarizes the stages of grieving.

CULTURAL DIVERSITY

An increasing number of students from culturally and linguistically diverse families are entering our special education classrooms. It is imperative as a special educator that you understand and accommodate for varying cultural perspectives of disabilities (Linan-Thompson & Jean, 1997).

Researchers suggest that teachers use the following strategies when collaborating with families from diverse cultural backgrounds (Cross, 1988; Huff & Telelsford, 1994; Lynch & Hanson, 1998):

1. Understand cultural differences and how they affect home–school interactions.
2. Acknowledge and adapt to differences in social etiquette and ways of expressing respect. Learn and use phrases of personal greetings.
3. Examine how a student's behavior may reflect cultural differences.
4. Adjust the collaboration process to validate and determine which activities may be appropriate.
5. Understand that the national emphasis on home–school collaboration may not mirror many countries' educational policies.
6. Locate cultural mentors or guides to facilitate your communication with families.
7. Include families in making decisions regarding their child's school program. Ask them to provide suggestions as to key phrases that would help their child become comfortable at your school.

FIGURE 10.1

Grieving State
Indicators and
Functions

Source: Adapted from
"The Impact of Childhood
Disability: The Parent's
Struggle," by Ken Moses,
1987, *Ways Magazine.*

Grieving State	Indicators	Function
Denial	• Sadness, confusion, helplessness • Crying or inappropriate laughter	Protects families from initial feelings of shock
Anxiety	• Anxiousness or agitation • Families may look for "miracle cure"	Catalyst for helping parents move forward in planning for child's future
Fear	• May appear overprotective	Encourages parents to reattach to their child and their dreams
Guilt	• Assume full responsibility for child's disability • Believe disability is punishment for their past misdeeds	Allows families to confront their loss and redefine the issue and cause of their child's disability
Depression	• Heavy sighing and/or crying • Detached and unresponsives	Allows families to come to terms with what it means to parent a child with a disability
Anger	• Projects responsibility for disability onto others • Shouts and is confrontational	Opens the way for exploration of the meaning of "justice" and "fairness" allows parents to move into making plans for their child's future

STEPS FOR COLLABORATING WITH PARENTS

Dettmer et al. (2005) suggest five basic steps for assisting teachers in the development of successful home–school partnerships, as described in the following subsections.

EXAMINE ONE'S OWN VALUES

- Explore your cultural connections and how your experiences shape your views of family, work ethic, life goals, behaviors, and communication style.
- The teacher's attitudes about diversity and the families' role in their child's education greatly affect the level of success of home–school partnerships.

BUILD COLLABORATIVE RELATIONSHIPS

- Use effective communication skills. Be an active listener and facilitate collaborative problem solving. Avoid educational jargon!
- Ask parents how they would like to communicate with you (e.g., phone, communication logs, face-to-face meetings).

▓ Support parents by giving them positive feedback for the efforts they are making in helping their child with homework, getting the child to school on time, and being a collaborative partner in their child's education.

▓ Provide parents with workshops on the curriculum you are using in your class. These workshops can be schoolwide or individually based. Provide translators as needed.

INITIATE HOME–SCHOOL INTERACTIONS

▓ Welcome parents into your classroom and provide them with opportunities to participate in meaningful activities such as reading to the class, helping prepare and/or implement art activities, and so on.

▓ Introduce new families to the school by providing them with a short orientation/tour of the school campus. Be sure they are introduced to all support services, paraprofessionals, and bus drivers as appropriate.

▓ Produce a weekly or monthly newsletter that describes current classroom activities, solicits parent involvement, and thanks parents for their participation.

▓ Create a bulletin board outside your classroom that showcases each family.

▓ Be aware of families' varying levels of need for participation and offer them choices of activities that include help both inside and outside of the classroom.

Figure 10.2 lists methods for staying in touch with families.

INDIVIDUALIZE FOR FAMILIES

▓ Avoid cultural stereotypes and generalizations regarding family structures.

▓ Familiarize yourself with each of your families and remember that all families are unique and do not fit a prescribed description.

▓ Provide families with a survey that identifies specific needs in the area of information on disabilities, the IEP process, community resources, and family support (see Figure 10.3).

EVALUATE HOME–SCHOOL COLLABORATION

▓ Evaluate your success in promoting home–school collaboration (see Figure 10.4).

▓ Remember that family collaboration should promote the strengths of the family and their unique contributions to the education of their child.

FIGURE 10.2

Mechanisms for Staying in Touch with Parents

- Daily notes
- Phone calls
- Weekly checklist
- Newsletters (teacher created)
- Class/program newspaper propject (student created)
- Class/program yearbook
- Web page

Need	Need Has Been Met	I Need Help with This
Information and Resources		
1. I need more information regarding my child's disability.		
2. I need more information on how to handle my child's behavior.		
3. I need more information on the IEP process.		
4. I need more information on parent rights.		
5. I need more information on services presently available for my child.		
6. I need more information about services my child might need in the future.		
Support		
1. I would like to have contact with other parents.		
2. I would like to have more contact with other parents of children with special needs.		
3. I would like more time to talk with my child's teacher.		
4. I would like more time to talk with my child's support-service providers.		
5. I would like more personal time to myself.		
6. I would like help in explaining my child's disability to other family members.		
7. I would like help in explaining my child's disability to other children.		
Community/Agency Services		
1. I would like help in finding day care or a preschool for my children.		
2. I would like help in locating a doctor or dentist for my child.		
3. I would like help locating babysitters or child-care providers who could care for my child.		
4. I would like help in finding funding for housing, food, medical care, child care, and/or transportation.		
5. I would like help in finding a job for myself or a family member.		
Please list any additional needs you might want addressed.		

FIGURE 10.3

Family Needs Survey

Source: Adapted from *Best Practices for Family Involvement in Comprehensive System of Personnel Development* (CSPD), 2000. California Department of Education Sacramento: CA.

FIGURE 10.4

Self-Assessment of
Building
Collaborative Family
Partnerships

Rate yourself on the following using this scale:
1 = never   2 = occasionally   3 = always

Collaborative Practice	Rating
1. I have examined my own cultural background and experiences.	
2. I understand how my own background and experiences shape my perceptions of diversity and home–school collaboration.	
3. I avoid using professional jargon when talking with families.	
4. I offer a variety of ways for families to communicate with me.	
5. I offer a variety of ways for families to participate in my classroom.	
6. I have established a variety of ways to show appreciation for my families' participation.	
7. I provide families with needed information and resources.	
8. I provide new families with a classroom/school orientation.	
9. I avoid cultural stereotypes and generalizations regarding family structures.	
10. I provide families with a needs survey that identifies specific areas of concern.	
11. I apply awareness of my families' individual strengths to strengthen my home-school partnerships.	

PARENT–TEACHER CONFERENCING

Parent conferences provide you with an opportunity to share information with families regarding their child's academic progress and social skills. Parent conferences are usually held on a schoolwide basis, across all grades and programs. Parent conferences are specifically designed to give periodic feedback to parents on their child's school performance. As a special educator, you may also need to schedule more informal and spontaneous meetings with parents to provide them with updates on their child's accomplishments or areas of concern.

PREPARING FOR PARENT CONFERENCES

In preparation for parent conferences, you will need to gather documentation of students' performance, schedule the conferences, and provide a comfortable place to meet. You will also need to implement effective communication strategies that will provide a foundation for a mutual sharing of ideas and concerns. Following are suggestions as to how to address these important components.

Scheduling

■ Encourage both parents to attend conferences whenever possible. However, be sensitive to the fact that many students are from nontraditional families. Many children live with grandparents, foster parents, stepparents, older siblings, or other adults. It may not always be the parent who is available to meet.

▓ Provide parents with several weeks' notice that the conference time is approaching. This can be accomplished through class newsletters or letters sent home. Use positive wording: "I'm looking forward to sharing your child's many accomplishments."

▓ Provide information on how and when parents may contact you about conferences.

▓ Schedule enough time for the meeting. Twenty to 30 minutes is usually adequate.

▓ When scheduling back-to-back conferences, allow enough time between each one (approximately 10 minutes) so that you can make notes on the just-concluded conference and prepare for the upcoming one.

▓ Give parents several choices for scheduling and be prepared to accommodate for evening or early morning appointments.

▓ Reminder calls or written notes the night before the conference are a good strategy for parents who have multiple work and family commitments.

Documentation

Have your papers organized in advance. Gather your gradebook, student test papers, samples of student work, attendance records, and other pertinent data ahead of time. Place the following in individual student folders:

▓ Past and current report cards
▓ Student work samples
▓ Samples of curriculum you are using
▓ Observation notes
▓ Progress charts on IEP goals and objectives

Be prepared to answer specific questions parents may have:

▓ What is my child's ability level?
▓ Is my child working up to his or her ability level?
▓ How is my child doing in specific subjects?
▓ Is my child disruptive?
▓ Do the other children like my child? Does he or she have friends?
▓ What does my child excel in?

MAKING PARENTS FEEL COMFORTABLE

▓ Provide parents who are waiting outside your door with chairs.
▓ Place a sign on your door that lets parents know you are in a conference and to wait outside until they are invited to come inside.
▓ Stay on schedule; don't make parents wait past their scheduled time.
▓ Greet parents warmly at the door.
▓ Sit at a comfortable table and provide comfortable chairs. Sit so you can easily maintain eye contact and share student work.

UTILIZING EFFECTIVE COMMUNICATION SKILLS

▓ Check your records ahead of time to make sure you know the parent's name. For example, don't assume that Julie Smith's mother is Mrs. Smith.
▓ Don't make the assumption that the elderly gentleman coming in with Johnny is his grandfather. It could be his father, or an uncle.

- Start with positive feedback, such as "Jack's smile always brightens my day" or "Julie has made great progess in the area of reading."

- Use specific feedback. Parents may be confused if you deal only in generalities. Instead of saying, "Omar doesn't accept responsibility," clarify the issue by pointing out "Omar had a whole week to finish his science report, but he only turned in two paragraphs."

- Offer a concrete action plan. Most parents appreciate being given specific direction. If Maria is immature, it might be helpful to suggest to her parents that they provide her with a list of weekly chores or that she take care of a pet. When you offer advice, let parents know you are only making suggestions and ask for their input.

- Practice patience and restraint. Although most parents will be open and respectful, some may be defensive or angry. Whatever the provocation, listen to parents calmly, without becoming defensive. If they do become verbally abusive during the meeting, calmly state that the meeting is over, immediately leave the room, and alert your administrator to the problem.

- Ask for parents' opinions. Let them know you are interested in working with them throughout the year to help make their child's education positive and successful. Allow ample time for parents to ask questions. Listen attentively and take notes.

- Focus on the student's strengths. Parents may feel defensive if they perceive their child's problem as a reflection on their parenting.

- Stress collaboration. Stating, "I'd like to discuss with you how we might work together to improve Laura's study skills," versus "You need to see me as soon as possible to discuss Laura's poor study skills," implies that you want to work together in the best interest of the child.

- Listen to what parents say. We often concentrate on what we are going to say next, lose concentration, or hear only part of what a speaker is saying. Truly listen to what parents are telling you.

- Ask parents if there is anything you should know about the child, such as health conditions, relationships with siblings, hobbies, or important events that may affect schoolwork.

- Focus on solutions. Some conferences will need to address specific student problems. Parents will be less defensive if you focus on solutions rather than on problems. Discuss what you can do together to improve the situation. Plan a course of action.

- Don't judge parents. Although some parents' values may be very different from your own, communicating your judgments of parents' attitudes or behaviors can be a roadblock to communication.

- Summarize the discussion and what actions you and the parents have decided to take at the end of the conference.

- Conclude the discussion on a positive note. Save at least one encouraging comment or positive statement about the student for the end of the conference.

- If you need more time, arrange another meeting.

- Parents will expect updates regarding any concerns or areas of improvement you have identified during the conference. Keep them informed!

- Keep a record of the conference. Make notes as soon as possible after the conference, while details are fresh. Maintain a separate file for each student.

- Record information regarding your communication with the student's parents throughout the school year. Regularly review the files to determine if follow-up communication is needed.

CULTURAL SENSITIVITY

Awareness and respect of your students' cultural backgrounds is crucial when scheduling and implementing parent conferences. It will be imperative to know whether families may require translators and to understand parents' cultural perceptions of their role in the education of their children. Your level of cross-cultural competence can help defuse potential misunderstandings and breaches of etiquette. It is important to remember that most families make decisions that are the best for their child. A family may not share your perception of what their child needs, but they will be more prone to follow through with an intervention that they value and support (Lynch & Hanson, 1998).

GUIDELINES FOR WORKING WITH AN INTERPRETER

There are several guidelines to follow when using an interpreter (Lynch & Hanson, 1998, pp. 82–83):

- Learn how to pronounce family names and memorize formal greetings in the family's native language.
- During the interaction, directly address your remarks and questions to the family, not the interpreter; look and listen to family members as they speak and observe their nonverbal communication.
- Avoid body language that may be offensive or misunderstood.
- Use a positive tone of voice and facial expressions. Address the family in a calm, unhurried way.
- Avoid educational jargon, colloquialisms, idioms, slang, and abstractions.
- Give instructions in a clear, logical sequence; emphasize key words or points; offer reasons for specific recommendations.
- Periodically check for the family's understanding and the accuracy of the translation by asking the family to repeat what has been communicated in their own words, but avoid literally asking, "Do you understand?"
- When possible, reinforce verbal information with materials written in the family's language and visual aids or modeling if appropriate.
- Be patient and prepared for the additional time it takes for careful interpretation.
- Avoid asking a student to act in the role of translator. Assuming this professional role can place the student in the awkward position of being perceived as being disrespectful of his or her elders and can cause discord within families.

CONFERENCING WITH GRANDPARENTS AND FOSTER CARE PROVIDERS

The 2000 U.S. Census placed the number of children living in a grandparent or other-relative-headed household at 6 million, and in 2005 over 500,000 children were cited as living in foster homes (U.S. Census Bureau, 2000; U.S. Department of Health and Human Services, 2005). Given this data, it is probable that you will be involved in a parent conference with either a grandparent and/or surrogate parent. Understanding the individual needs of each of these populations will help to create a more positive and productive conference.

Grandparents

Grandparents may be keeping families together and may be keeping their grandchildren out of the formal foster care system. Grandparents may face many obstacles (see Figure 10.5).

FIGURE 10.5

Did You Know?

> Grandparents may assume the role of parenting for a number of reasons:
>
> - Substance abuse
> - Death of a parent
> - Child abuse
> - Abandonment
> - Teen pregnancy
> - HIV/AIDS
> - Unemployment
> - Incarceration
> - Divorce
> - Mental health issues
> - Family violence
> - Poverty

Unless grandparents are the legal guardians of their grandchildren, they may be unable to:

- Place the children on their health-care insurance policies
- Obtain affordable housing in which they can live with the children
- Enroll the children in school or sign IEPs

Some grandparents ask the courts to make them legal guardians for the grandchild they are raising. This allows the grandparents to make important decisions for the child. Some states won't allow a grandparent to enroll a child in school or participate in school conferences unless the grandparent has legal custody. Before scheduling conferences you will need to establish whether the grandparents are the legal guardians of your student. If they are not legal guardians they may need permission from the legal guardian to attend the conference. It is your responsibility to ascertain what legal rights the grandparents have in participating in their grandchild's education. Your school psychologist or the child's social worker should be able to help you with this determination.

Foster Care Providers

Once again, you will need a clear understanding of which of your students may be in foster care and which foster parents may be attending your parent conferences. Under federal law, every child in foster care must be appointed an educational liaison. The foster parent is responsible for making normal parenting decisions such as choosing recreational activities and attending school functions. Their educational responsibilities also include:

- Ensuring proper school placement; enrolling and checking out the student from school
- Assisting in transfer of grades, credits, and records

Under certain circumstances, the foster parent has educational rights with respect to consenting to the IEP and related educational program. It is your responsibility to determine your state's mandates in regard to the educational rights and responsibilities of foster parents. Consulting with your student's social worker will provide you with valuable information and insights into these rights and responsibilities.

Strategies for Including Parents in Decision Making

Including families in the decision making leading up to an IEP or IFSP meeting is a challenging but necessary process. Lack of parent input into the development of their child's IEP may lead to dissatisfaction with special education services. The following subsections describe factors to consider when involving parents in the IEP and IFSP decision-making process.

Before and During the Assessment Process

- Assessment procedures and parent rights have been explained to the family in their primary language.
- Observations have taken place in a variety of settings, including social settings and the home.
- A parent inventory has been completed that lists the parents' goals for their child.
- Assessment instruments have been selected that address cultural and linguistic biases.

Before the IEP/IFSP Meeting

- Professional translators are available to facilitate communication.
- Meeting schedules have remained flexible to accommodate parents' needs.
- Parents' legal rights have been explained.
- Parents are aware of local support groups and resources.
- IEP protocols and processes have been carefully explained.
- Family has participated in the development of their child's IEP goals/objectives prior to the meeting (based on information provided in a parent inventory).
- All assessment information has been reviewed with the family.
- Information and protocols have been provided in the family's primary language.
- Parents are familiar with where and when the meeting is being held and have transportation as needed.

During the IEP Meeting

- Professional translators are available to facilitate communication.
- Family is greeted warmly and is seated close to familiar people.
- All assessment forms and legal documents are in the family's primary language.
- Professionals use informal language and avoid jargon when conducting the meeting.
- Culturally sensitive issues such as nonverbal and verbal communication are respected by all participants.
- Family is encouraged to participate in the process and express their ideas and/or concerns.
- Facilitator stops and checks for understanding frequently during the meeting.

FIGURE 10.6
Take a Moment

Think About	Reflect	Respond
Partnerships with parents	What is your position on the benefits of family involvement for your students' education? Does family involvement benefit the education of your students? Why or why not?	
	How much does your understanding of your students' cultural backgrounds and experiences influence your ability to provide appropriate curriculum and instruction?	
	How much does awareness of your own cultural background and experiences shape your interactions with your students' families?	

AFTER THE IEP MEETING

- Contact the parents the day after the meeting for questions or concerns and respond to them as soon as possible.
- Continue to maintain contact with families regarding the progress their child is making toward the established goals/objectives.
- Continue to solicit information as to how their child is doing in the home environment and community.
- Continue to offer resources and support as needed.

Figure 10.6 asks you to reflect on relationships with parents.

CONCLUSION

Family involvement is a significant variable in the development of a child. Past and present legislation has underscored the importance of home–school connections and has mandated family involvement in all aspects of educational decision making. As a special educator you will provide the foundation for bridging the home–school connection by providing clear pathways for communication, valuing families' unique strengths, and providing support as they experience the grief and challenges and joys of raising a child with exceptionalities.

The United States is one of the most culturally, ethnically, and linguistically diverse nations (Friend & Cook, 2003). Understanding your cultural perspectives and those of your families will be paramount to success in building collaborative partnerships with families and will help guide you through the often turbulent but always rewarding process of forming relationships.

EXPLORATIONS

1. Create a handbook for families of the children in your classroom. What supports would they need in order become active members of your home–school collaboration?

2. Conduct an informal interview with a family member of a student with exceptionalities. Ask him or her to reflect on experiences with the IEP process. What has been positive and negative about the family member's experiences? What suggestions does he or she have for improving communication between home and school?

3. Providing support and services for families from diverse backgrounds is essential to forming collaborative partnerships. What resources are necessary in order to address the specific needs of your families?

WEBSITES

Beach Center on Disability

http://www.beachcenter.org

This site provides current research and fact sheets on a variety of topics of interest for families and professionals. It offers focused information in the areas of educational, vocational, and adult living issues.

Family Voices

http://www.familyvoices.org

This site is a national clearinghouse for information on health care of children with exceptionalities. It includes a bimonthly newsletter, news updates, and publications.

National Information Center for Children and Youth with Disabilities (NICHCY)

http://www.nichcy.org

This site acts as a referral center that provides information on disabilities and related issues for families and professionals. Many features are available in Spanish.

Parents Helping Parents

http://www.php.com

This site provides comprehensive resources for parents and is created and maintained by parents.

REFERENCES

Chen, D., McLean, M., Corso, R., & Bruns, D. (2001). *Working together in EI: Cultural considerations in helping relationships and service utilization.* (Technical Report No. 11). [electronic version]. Champaign-Urbana, IL: Culturally and Linguistically Appropriate Services for Early Childhood Research (CLAS) Institute.

Christenson, S. L., & Cleary, M. (1990). Consultation and the parent-education partnership: A perspective. *Journal of Educational and Psychological Consultation, 1,* 219–241.

Cross, T. (1988). Services to minority populations: What does it mean to be a culturally competent professional? *Focal Point, 2,* 1–3.

Dettmer, P., Thurston, L., & Dyck, M. (2005). *Consultation, collaboration, and teamwork for students with special needs.* Boston, MA: Pearson Ed. Inc.

Friend, M., & Cook, L. (2003). *Ineteractions: Collaboration Skills for school professionals.* (4th ed.). Boston: Allyn & Bacon.

Hansen, J. C., Himes, B. S., & Meier, S. (1990). *Consultation: Concepts and practices.* Upper Saddle River, NJ: Prentice Hall.

Huff, B., & Telesford, M. C. (1994). Outreach efforts to involve families of color in the Federation of Families for Children's Mental Health. *Focal Point, 10,* 180–184.

Linan-Thompson, S., & Jean, R. (1997). Completing the parent participation puzzle: Accepting diversity. *Teaching Exceptional Children, 30*(2), 46–50.

Lynch, E., & Hanson, M. (1998). *Developing cross-cultural competence* (2nd ed.). Baltimore, MD: Paul Brookes Publishing Co.

Moses, K. (1987). The impact of childhood disability: The parent's struggle. *Ways Magazine.* 4–7.

Turnbull, E., Rothstein-Fisch, C., Greenfield, P. M., & Quiroz, B. (2001). *Bridging cultures between home and school: A guide for teachers.* Mahwah, NJ: Erlbaum.

U.S. Census Bureau. (2000). Population survey. Available online at *http://www.census.gov/population/www/socdemo/grandparents.*

U.S. Department of Health and Human Services. (2005). Trends in foster care and adoption, FY 2000–FY 2005. Available online at *http://www.acf.hhs.gov/programs/cb/stats_research/afcars/sec11gb/.*

11

Survival to Success: Stress Reduction and Time Management Strategies

"Knowledge is not a goal in itself, but a path to wisdom; it bestows not privilege so much as duty, not power so much as responsibility. And it brings with it a desire to learn even as one teaches, to teach even as one learns. It is used not to compete with one's fellow beings for some unending standard of life, but to achieve for them, as for oneself, a higher quality of life."

A. Sivanandan

CHAPTER OBJECTIVES

- Provide practical tips for coping with stress
- Present time management techniques to achieve personal and professional goals
- Present activities to sustain continuous professional development

Before reading this chapter, note what comes to mind when you think of effective special education teachers. Effective special education teachers are those who are mentally healthy, take care of their own needs, and develop positive relationships with others. Do you feel stressed and overwhelmed? How well do you manage your time at work and at home? How can better time management help you? Record your reflections and revisit your response as you read this chapter.

INTRODUCTION

"Every year, U.S. schools hire more than 200,000 new teachers for the first day of school. By the time summer rolls around, at least 22,000 have quit" (Graziano, 2005, p. 40). According to Graziano (2005, p. 40), about 30% of new teachers leave the profession after just 3 years, and more than 45% leave after 5 years. Currently, 37% of the teaching workforce is over age 50 and considering retirement. Special educators, in particular, are more likely to leave the classroom due to the stress caused by the unmanageability of their workload (Brownell, 2005). Brownell (1997, p. 1) states, "The ability to successfully manage stresses related to teaching is critical if special education teachers are to survive and thrive in the classroom." This chapter provides strategies for coping with stress in the special education classroom, emphasizing personal time management techniques and professional development activities. Before reading further, use Figure 11.1 to reflect on stress in your work environment.

FIGURE 11.1
Take a Moment

Think About	Reflect	Respond
Stress in your work	Do you feel tense and insecure?	
	Do you have guilty feelings about not doing a better job? Is your job fun?	

PRACTICAL TIPS FOR COPING WITH STRESS

SOURCES OF STRESS

Sometimes it is difficult to remember that not all stress is bad. According to Davis, Eshelman, and McKay (2000, p. 1), "Stress is an everyday fact of life. You can't avoid it. Stress is any change that you must adapt to, ranging from the negative extreme of actual physical danger to the exhilaration of falling in love or achieving some long desired success. . . . In fact, stress is not only desirable but also essential to life." Regardless of the stress that you experience, it is the manner in which you respond to stress that determines the impact that it will have on your job, daily activities, and life in general. Four major sources of stress, adapted from Davis et al. (2000), are:

1. Social and job stressors such as deadlines, finances, job and family demands on your time and attention, loss of loved ones, interpersonal conflict, and poor time management.
2. Environmental stressors such as weather, noise, pollution, cramped space, and lack of structure or order.
3. Physiological stressors such as lack of sleep, lack of exercise, poor nutrition, illness, injuries, and aging.
4. Thought stressors such as how your brain interprets and reacts to changes in your environment and body, which sometimes triggers a "physical emergency response."

Because gaining awareness of the causes of stress and coming to the realization that the key to reducing stress comes from your response to it is essential to reducing stress, the following strategies are offered to help you "take your job and love it" (Council for Exceptional Children, 2004).

DEALING WITH ROLE OVERLOAD

As a special education teacher, role overload is one of the major sources of stress that contributes to the feeling of being overwhelmed. Not only are you performing the duties of a teacher who is responsible for an entire class or caseload, you may also be involved in a rigorous academic teacher preparation program at the same time. Your role as parent, spouse, sibling, and daughter or son also requires time and attention. Sometimes you may feel like you are being pulled in so many directions that you are not able to do your best at any one task. The following strategies are offered to help you alleviate some of the stress caused by role overload.

Set Realistic Expectations

One way to reduce stress as a special education teacher is to set realistic expectations for yourself. A major part of your teaching responsibility is to identify the learning needs of your students and write individualized education programs. Sometimes this activity translates into the notion that being a successful teacher means that you have the ability to solve all of your students' problems. It is important to remember that this is not always possible, particularly for beginning special educators. "To competently manage the challenging, diverse needs of students with disabilities, professionals need to perform at a high level in the areas of curriculum, behavior management, instructional management, collaboration, and paperwork. Attempting perfection in each of these areas, especially early in your career, may be unrealistic" (Brownell, 2000, p. 2). Brownell further suggests that the best way to approach this situation is to target only one area for improvement over the year and to learn as much as possible through reading, taking courses, attending conferences, or sharing with your colleagues.

Plan and Prioritize Daily Tasks

One way to reduce the amount of stress from role overload is to give yourself 10 minutes each day, either in the evening, morning, or during your lunch break, to write down the tasks or activities that you need to complete for the next day, including both professional and personal activities and/or tasks. The next step is to prioritize the tasks according to what is important to you personally, as well as to your program's administrator. Prioritize the tasks according to the coding system in Figure 11.2 by writing a number next to each daily task.

Next, tackle these tasks in the order of importance by first completing all tasks with the number 1. If time permits, complete the tasks coded with the number 2. If time doesn't permit, place the tasks coded with number 2 on your next day's list of prioritized tasks. During your specified planning time, prioritize all your next day's activities accordingly using the coding system in Figure 11.2. As you plan and prioritize for the next day, be sure to look at the next day with a new perspective. Given all the tasks that need to be completed tomorrow, what are your priorities? In other words, it is like "refreshing" your computer screen. Each day takes on a perspective unto itself. Some tasks that appeared as a number 1 on one day may need to be coded as a number 2 the next day. Over time, and with improved planning, the list of daily tasks will become shorter and the process of prioritization will become clearer to you. Eventually, you will be able to look at your tasks for the week ahead and write down what needs to be completed on each day of the week and then prioritize each day's tasks with the coding system.

The key to successful planning and reducing role overload is to limit, as much as possible, the amount of tasks that need to be completed on any given day. In our "information" day and age, there is a general unrealistic expectation about what can be accomplished successfully by one person in one day. As a result, special education teachers tend to "pack" the day with too many high-priority tasks. This results in increased stress and feelings of being overwhelmed because you are not able to accomplish all of the day's high-priority tasks in a timely manner. This is why taking the time to plan and prioritize your daily tasks is so critical to your well-being and job success.

FIGURE 11.2

Coding System for Prioritizing Tasks

1 = Critically important and must be completed today

2 = Critically important and can be done tomorrow

3 = Not so important and can be done in the next few days

Balance Your Job and Your Personal Life

As a special education teacher, you are educating students with special needs and complex challenges. Not only are you providing direct instruction to students, but you are also working intensely with other adults all of the time. As a consultant and collaborator, you have additional job duties and demands. According to Brownell (2000, p. 2), "Being able to show empathy for students and their problems without allowing those problems to consume you is critical." One strategy for addressing role overload is to consciously leave thoughts of your workday interactions between students and other adults at school and not carry them home into your personal life. If you feel a need to share your feelings and frustrations, plan a time to meet with a colleague and/or friend to discuss issues. Brownell (2000, p. 2) suggests that "when you discuss frustrations, you should try to find solutions to the stressful situations. Repeated discussion about your frustrations without any solution only heightens them."

Increase Teaching Confidence

Increasing your teaching confidence and perceiving yourself as having the tools to do your job successfully can minimize stress induced by role overload. Evidence of your efforts is apparent in your students' progress. Implementing best practices in your classroom and monitoring your students' progress can directly relate to increased teaching confidence, and thus lower your stress levels. We do caution you, however, that lack of student progress does not necessarily indicate shortcomings on your part. Students with special needs face multiple challenges daily. We encourage you to do what is required and to address your students' learning needs on a daily basis, but to also realize that you cannot do it all.

Use Professional Judgment

In the role of advocate for students and the profession, many special education teachers become disappointed and discouraged with the multiple levels of bureaucratic impediments and inflexibility found in their working environment. Rules may seem inflexible, but many times they are open to interpretation. As an advocate for your students and your profession, use your professional judgment to first identify changes that will improve your environment and then focus your energy on creating the changes that are within your control. This process helps you to increase your sense of autonomy and reduce your stress levels. Join professional organizations in order to work with others who share your desire for changes to improve working conditions for teachers. This is an example of a direct active strategy to deal with professional stress. Direct and indirect active strategies for coping with stress are discussed in further detail in the next section of this chapter.

COPING STRATEGIES

Strategies to cope with stress include direct active strategies and indirect active strategies. The research on stress suggests that direct active strategies are more effective (Brownell, 2000).

DIRECT ACTIVE STRATEGIES

When you use direct active strategies, you can change the source of your stress, confront the source of your stress, or change your response to the source of your stress. A direct active strategy to change the source of your stress is to change the nature of the stressful situation. For example, if you perceive that the principal in your school is not supporting the inclusion of students with special needs in the general education classroom, you could focus on including only one student with a particular general education teacher who welcomes this student and work with him or her to implement a successful inclusive classroom experience. By changing the source of the stressful situation from the lack of support from the principal to the increase in support from the general education teacher, you have reduced your professional stress and also created a meaningful learning environment for one of your students.

Confronting the source of stress means dealing directly with the source of the stress. An example of this approach occurs when you directly discuss a problem with a student or colleague. For example, when there is a problem working with your paraprofessional, set a specific time to discuss this issue with the intent of jointly resolving the situation. This direct active strategy confronts the source of the stress in a productive manner, resulting in a reduction of stress for both you and your paraprofessional.

Changing your response to the source of your stress is another strategy for stress reduction. Of course, this strategy makes a great deal of sense because in terms of control, you have more control over yourself and your attitude than you do over any other person or situation. When you are positive and try to have a cheerful and accepting attitude, and give others in your environment positive feedback, you can change how you perceive stress and thus cope with stressful events in a better manner. This applies to your attitude with other adults as well as students in your working environment. A positive outlook is contagious and other individuals, of all ages, will want to be around you and support you. Developing support is considered an indirect active strategy and will be presented in the next section.

INDIRECT ACTIVE STRATEGIES

Indirect active strategies reduce stress by either releasing it or engaging in activities known to reduce it. The literature on stress is full of lists of stress reducers that highlight indirect active strategies. For instance, Dr. Andrew Weil (1996, p. 2), an integrative medicine specialist, outlines eight steps to stress relief. These steps exemplify indirect active strategies and are as follows (Reproduced with permission from *Dr. Andrew Weil's Self Healing* newsletter. Subscriptions from (800)523-3296. Copyright 2007 by Body & Soul Omnimedia, Inc).

1. Remove obstacles to relaxation by avoiding caffeine, chocolate, over-the-counter drugs that make you jumpy and anxious, a steady diet of conflict presented by the media, loud music on the car radio, and the company of people who are chronically angry or agitated.
2. Pay attention to your breath because breathing has a direct connection to your emotional state.
3. Practice a regular form of exercise because this is one of the most important things you can do to manage stress. You might want to plan your workout around the most anxious part of your day: Some studies suggest that those who feel more tense during the workday benefit most from a morning workout, and those who lie awake sleepless are better off exercising in the late afternoon.
4. Try meditation to relax the body and quiet the mind.
5. Laugh it off because laughter provides real health benefits, boosting the immune function of the body. The average 6-year-old laughs 300 times a day; the average adult laughs 17 times a day. Seek out people who share your sense of humor, particularly at work.

FIGURE 11.3

Building Stress
Reduction Cues in
the Teaching
Environment

Source: Developed by
Mary C. Jensen, Ph.D.,
California State
University—Chico,
Chico, CA.

Visual cues	Posters, art prints of relaxing scenes, calming colors; teacher dress style; reminders for YOU, posted in your teaching line of vision
Auditory cues	Baroque or environmental music; sound boxes
Ambience cues	Scents, flowers, lights
Informal teacher cues—ways to relax a situation	Teacher slowed breathing, slowed walk, slowed speech, calming gestures, attentiveness

6. Build a strong social network to buffer the effects of stress. Many special education teachers have mentors or support providers selected by their districts and/or university preparation programs to provide support and assistance as a part of teacher professional induction. We strongly encourage you to seek the company and expertise of your mentor. Engage in personal and professional activities together to establish and maintain your professional support network and reduce the stress created by professional teaching isolation.

7. Boost resilience to stress nutritionally. A good daily antioxidant formula protects immune function, providing greater resilience in the face of stress. The antioxidant regimen I recommend is 200 to 250 mg of vitamin C, 400 IU of vitamin E as natural mixed tocopherols (or 80 mg as mixed tocopherols and tocotrienols), 200 mcg of the mineral selenium, and 10,000 to 15,000 IU of mixed carotenoids (or 10,000 IU of beta-carotene). You might also start taking a tonic suitable for long-term use, such as Siberian ginseng. Take in a tincture or capsule form according to the manufacturer's directions.

8. Seek professional help if you can't neutralize your stress with the self-care techniques just outlined.

Another indirect active strategy for reducing stress for students and the teacher that directly applies to the special education classroom is the utilization of stress reduction cues in the teaching environment (see Figure 11.3).

An additional resource of 52 proven tips for reducing stress from the Hope Heart Institute is provided in Figure 11.4. The research continuously points to time management as a means of effectively reducing stress. Therefore, due to its importance, especially for those individuals who are in the special education profession, a separate section on time management techniques to achieve personal and professional goals is presented next.

TIME MANAGEMENT TECHNIQUES TO ACHIEVE GOALS

Time management means the efficient use of resources, including time, in such a way that we are effective in achieving important personal goals. Efficiency has been defined as doing things right—effectiveness has been defined as doing the *right* things right. The first step to effectively manage your time is to assess how you use your time and how you would like to use it. Figure 11.5 provides a time log to help you analyze your time usage.

1. Get up 15 minutes earlier in the morning.

2. Prepare for the morning the evening before.

3. Don't rely on your memory. Write down appointment times, meetings, birthdays, etc.

4. Do nothing that, after being done, leads you to tell a lie.

5. Make duplicates of all keys.

6. Practice preventative maintenance.

7. Eliminate (or restrict) the amount of caffeine in your diet.

8. Procrastination is stressful. Whatever you want to do tomorrow, do today; whatever you want to do today, do now.

9. Plan ahead.

10. Don't put up with something that doesn't work right.

11. Allow 15 minutes of extra time to get to appointments.

12. Be prepared to wait. Bring a book!

13. Always set up contingency plans, "just in case."

14. Relax your standards.

15. Pollyanna power! For every one thing that goes wrong, there are many more things to appreciate.

16. Ask questions. Clarification can save you much time and stress.

17. Say, "No!"

18. Unplug your phone when you want uninterrupted time.

19. Turn "needs" into preferences.

20. Simplify, simplify, simplify.

21. Make friends with nonworriers.

22. Take a hot bath or shower (or a cool one, in summertime) to relieve tension.

23. Wear earplugs if you need quiet at home and it is not possible.

24. Get enough sleep.

25. Create order out of chaos. Organize your home and workspace so that you always know exactly where things are placed.

26. Check your breathing throughout the day. Short, shallow breaths indicate stress. Take several deep, slow breaths to relax.

27. Write down your thoughts and feelings in a journal to gain a new perspective.

28. To relax, perform a yoga technique. Inhale deeply through your nose to a count of 8. Then with lips puckered, exhale through your mouth to the count of 16 while you sigh. Repeat 10 times.

(continued)

FIGURE 11.4

Fifty-two Proven Tips for Reducing Stress

Source: Adapted from the Hope Heart Institute, Seattle, WA.

29. Innoculate yourself against a feared event by practicing, practicing, practicing.

30. Use diversion, or a change in activity or environment, to get a job done when the stress of having to get it done gets in the way.

31. Get up and stretch periodically if you sit for extended periods of time.

32. Select an environment (home, work, leisure) that is in line with your personal needs and desires.

33. Learn to live one day at a time.

34. Every day, do something you really enjoy.

35. Add an ounce of love to everything that you do.

36. Talk it out.

37. Do something for somebody else.

38. Focus on understanding rather than on being understood, on loving rather than on being loved.

39. Do something that will improve your appearance. Looking better can help you feel better.

40. Schedule a realistic day. Avoid the tendency to schedule back-to-back appointments; allow time between appointments for a breathing spell.

41. Become more flexible. Some things are not worth doing perfectly and on some issues it is okay to compromise.

42. Eliminate destructive self-talk: "I'm too old to . . ." "I'm too fat to . . ."

43. Use your weekend time for a change of pace.

44. Take care of today's tasks as best you can, and the yesterdays and tomorrows will take care of themselves.

45. Do one thing at a time.

46. Allow yourself time—every day—for privacy, quiet, and introspection.

47. If an especially "unpleasant" task faces you, do it early in the day and get it over with. Then the rest of your day will be free of anxiety.

48. Learn to delegate responsibility to capable others.

49. Don't forget to take a lunch break.

50. Be sure to count to 20 before doing something or saying anything that could make matters worse.

51. Have a forgiving view of events and people. Accept the fact that we live in an imperfect world.

52. Have an optimistic view of the world. Believe that most people are doing the best they can.

FIGURE 11.4

(continued)

The next step is to identify time problems by analyzing the causes that keep you from achieving your ideal amount of time in any of the activities listed in the first column in Figure 11.5. The time management literature refers to time wasters as *time robbers* or *time bandits*. In our guide, we refer to time wasters as *time stealers*. Figure 11.6 outlines common time stealers. Review Figure 11.6 and note if the cause of your time problems stems from any common time stealers.

Directions: Review the list of activities in the first column. Fill in the amount of time that you presently use on the activities (as a percentage), as well as the ideal amount of time that you would like to spend on the activities (as a percentage).

1) PERSONAL/WORK	PRESENT AMOUNT OF TIME = _____ %	IDEAL AMOUNT OF TIME = _____ %
a. Eating		
b. Sleeping		
c. Dressing		
d. Commuting to work		
e. Family/household chores (specify)		
2) ON-THE-JOB	PRESENT AMOUNT OF TIME = _____ %	IDEAL AMOUNT OF TIME = _____ %
a. Important projects		
b. Catching up with routine projects		
c. Nonproductive activities		
3) TIME WITH FAMILY	PRESENT AMOUNT OF TIME = _____ %	IDEAL AMOUNT OF TIME = _____ %
4) PERSONAL GROWTH	PRESENT AMOUNT OF TIME = _____ %	IDEAL AMOUNT OF TIME = _____ %
5) LEISURE	PRESENT AMOUNT OF TIME = _____ %	IDEAL AMOUNT OF TIME = _____ %
6) ALONE TIME (Time by Myself)	PRESENT AMOUNT OF TIME = _____ %	IDEAL AMOUNT OF TIME = _____ %
7) FREE TIME (Unscheduled Time)	PRESENT AMOUNT OF TIME = _____ %	IDEAL AMOUNT OF TIME = _____ %

FIGURE 11.5

The Time Log: Analysis of Your Time Usage

Managing your time means managing yourself, and that means managing your personal resources, or strengths. Therefore, the third step in the process of effective time management is to assess your personal resources. A Personal Resource Assessment (Figure 11.7) is provided for you to begin to think about what important personal resources you bring to your work, family, community, and yourself. It is also valuable to have an understanding of your personal resources or assets as you begin to think about your personal and professional development goals.

Inherent in the concept of allocating resources is purpose. Therefore the next step is to identify personal and professional development goals and a projected timeline for completing them. Clearly stating your goals enables you to better manage your time and brings you closer to attaining those goals. Therefore, as you write your personal goals

Common Time
Stealers

Internal Time Stealers	External Time Stealers
• Poor planning	• Meetings
• Failure to listen	• Waiting for answers
• Unclear goals	• Socializing
• Lack of self-discipline	• Interruptions
• Unreal time estimates	• Peer demands
• Poor communication	• Red tape
• Lack of motivation	• Equipment failure
• Negative attitude	• Cluttered workspace
• Overinvolvement with details	• Lack of procedures
• Lack of delegation	• Mistakes of others
• Mistakes—my own	• Unwanted mail
• Unwillingness to say no	
• Overcommitment	
• Indecision	
• Procrastination	

Personal Resource
Assessment

Think about the personal resources that you bring to your work, family, community, and self by answering the following questions:

1) What are the personal resources that you bring to your work? (examples: experience, training, motivation, creativity, leadership qualities)

2) What are the personal resources that are important to your family? (examples: financial, love, moral values)

3) What are the personal resources that are important in your community or school or volunteer work? (examples: leadership skills, concern for individuals with disabilities)

4) What are the personal resources that give you inward satisfaction? (examples: an interest in music, a strong pitch, a knowledge of plants and trees)

using Figure 11.8, be sure that your goal statements are specific, measurable, action oriented, realistic, and timely (Smith, 1994). The following example is provided to help you write your personal goals: *By one year from today, I will have completed all of my coursework for my Special Education credential through an approved State Certification Program.*

As a special educator, organizing your time and your activities to achieve your professional goals is critical. Setting realistic and flexible personal and professional goals and objectives will make it possible to accomplish them. On the other hand, be cautious not to set your goals too low, resulting in a lack of motivation for you. Once you have established goals for yourself, prioritize these goals in terms of importance and feasibility. Look

FIGURE 11.8

Personal Goal
Writing

Write your PERSONAL GOALS in this column (Remember: Goals need to be specific, measurable, action oriented, realistic, and timely to be meaningful.)	Check this column if you intend to achieve this goal in this year.	Check this column if you intend to achieve this goal in the longer term.
Work goals:		
Family goals:		
Community goals:		
Self goals:		

FIGURE 11.9

Take a Moment

Think About	Reflect	Respond
How are you spending your time and living your life?	Are you spending your time the way you really want to spend it?	
	Do you feel obligated to do too many things you really don't want to do?	
	Do you get a feeling of self-satisfaction and accomplishment from your work?	
	Do you take work home on evenings and weekends?	
	Do you feel overwhelmed with all of the different tasks that you are required to do?	
	Do you have time to keep physically fit?	

at the "big picture." What goals are realistically attainable while you are teaching full time and managing your home life? Be sure to pace yourself. Take small steps on a daily, weekly, and yearly basis to achieve your goals. Develop an action plan for yourself that includes professional growth activities directly related to your identified goals. Use Figure 11.9 to reflect on your personal goals and time management.

ACTIVITIES TO SUSTAIN CONTINUOUS PROFESSIONAL DEVELOPMENT

Professional and personal growth requires that you keep learning. One way to do this is by taking additional coursework. Select courses that interest you and align with your personal and professional goals. Distance learning options, including computer-based online Web courses, provide a convenient way to obtain new skills and information.

Another means to gain new knowledge and foster professional relationships is to join at least one professional organization (see Figure 11.10). Professional organizations typically distribute the most current information to their members using newsletters, journals, magazines, and/or Web sites. Furthermore, professional organizations usually hold state and national annual conferences. We strongly recommend that you plan to attend at least one professional conference each year as part of your professional growth activities. Planning ahead for such an event will help you to get the needed support for you to enjoy your conference experience and reduce the stress associated with leaving your classroom and home for a brief time period.

A third way to nurture your professional growth is to read professional journals and books on a regular basis to remain current in your field. Most schools have professional lending libraries, but if this is not available to you, the Internet provides a convenient means for you to access electronic journals and order professional books and resources.

Sustaining your professional growth directly relates to your effectiveness as a special education teacher and your ability to best serve individuals with disabilities. It helps to increase your teaching confidence and capability, reduce professional isolation, and contribute to your well-being as a successful special education professional. Figure 11.11 asks you to reflect on continuous professional development.

FIGURE 11.10

Examples of Professional Organization Web Sites

American Association on Intellectual and Developmental Disabilities (AAIDD): *www.aamr.org*

American Council of the Blind: *www.acb.org*

American Federation of Teachers: *www.aft.org*

American Speech-Language-Hearing Association: *www.asha.org*

ARC of the United States: *www.thearc.org*

Autism Society of America: *www.autism-society.org*

Council for Exceptional Children: *www.cec.sped.org*

National Association of Early Childhood Teacher Educators (NAECTE): *www.naecte.org*

National Down Syndrome Society: *www.ndss.org*

National Education Association (NEA): *www.nea.org*

United Cerebral Palsy: *www.ucpa.org*

FIGURE 11.11

Take a Moment

Think About	Reflect	Respond
Continuous Professional Development	Do you have a method for continuing your professional growth and development?	

CONCLUSION

Stress reduction and time management are critical skill areas for special educators. Juggling the demands of home, work, and school is incredibly stressful and produces a feeling of being overwhelmed. This chapter presents practical tips for coping with stress and a process to help you manage your time more effectively to achieve your personal and professional goals. Strategies for professional growth and development are included to help you to sustain your enthusiasm for teaching and encourage your continuous professional development.

Moving from "survival" to "success" can be achieved by giving yourself the gift of mindful planning and preparation as you complete your teacher certification program and enter your first year of teaching special education. Remember to be kind, gentle, and accepting of yourself as you make this unique professional journey. Keep in mind that the first year is always the most difficult. The learning curve is steep—but it does get better. Making a difference in the lives of the children whom you teach is one of the major reasons that special education teachers remain in the profession. In a recent teacher retention study by Dr. Ken Futernick (2007), 65% of the special education teachers who responded to an electronic survey reported staying in special education because they feel that they make a difference in their students' lives. His report (2007, pp. 39–40) captures the voice of one special educator who explained

> The most important factors influencing my decision to stay in teaching in general and special education in particular are the beliefs, reinforcement, and validation that I am making a positive difference in the lives of the students I teach. That does not mean that my students only "perform" based on state standards, but that I have a daily (and I hope lifelong) positive impact on outcomes for these students— whether these outcomes are social, emotional, vocational, or educational. . . . Knowing that I have reached a level of competence, confidence, and expertise in working with students has helped me become proud of my career choice—even in discouraging times.

EXPLORATIONS

1. Think about role overload. One suggestion for reducing stress is to set realistic expectations for yourself and to identify one area that you would like to focus on for improvement. What area would you like to focus on in the next year?

2. Planning and prioritizing your daily activities is key to reducing stress. For 10 days, take 10 minutes each day to write down the tasks that you need to complete the next day and prioritize them using the coding system presented in Figure 11.2. Check off the tasks after you complete them. After 10 days, assess your stress level. Were you able to complete your daily tasks in a timely manner? Did you reduce the feeling of being overwhelmed? Are you beginning to get a better handle on this process of planning and prioritizing your daily tasks?

3. Review the coping strategies covered in this chapter, both direct and indirect. Select one strategy or tip that you feel will benefit you in your daily work. Describe why you think it will benefit you.

4. Use the time management techniques presented in this chapter to create an individualized professional development plan by first writing your professional development goal for next year. (Remember to consider your personal resources as you write your goal.) Second, produce an action plan for achieving this goal by writing three

professional growth activities that will help you to achieve your goal. Prioritize your three activities and be sure to include a target date by which you plan to complete each professional growth activity. Provide a space to check off your activities as you complete them next year.

WEBSITES

Association for Supervision and Curriculum Development (ACSD)
http://www.ascd.org/services/eric/facts.html
This professional organizational site provides selected abstracts on current educational issues.

Council for Exceptional Children (CEC)
http://www.cec.sped.org
This professional organizational site provides multiple resources for the special educator to stay current in the field.

Federal Resources for Educational Excellence
http://www.ed.gov/free
This site offers free resources for educators.

MIT Online Learning Modules: Time Management and Organization
http://mit.edu/arc/learning/modules/time/
This site offers a list of simple ways to save time as well as a process for a well-balanced schedule. The site is designed to assist university students to better manage their time.

Stressbusting Stress Relief Management
http://stressbusting.co.uk
This site provides numerous resources for dealing with stress, including an assessment that yields an SQ or stress quotient, ways of coping with stress, and 10 tips for busting stress.

Stress Management—Topic Overview
http://www.webmd.com/hw/emotional_wellness/hw153409.asp
This site offers short articles on stress and time management.

U.S. Department of Education
http://www.ed.gov/offices/OERI/ECI
This site provides current legal information for the practicing professional teacher.

U.S. Department of Education
http://www.ed/gov/pubs/FirstYear
This site provides information on what to expect your first year of teaching.

REFERENCES

Billingsley, B. S. (2003). *Special education teacher retention and attrition: A critical analysis of the literature.* (COPSSE Document Number RS-2). Gainesville: University of Florida, Center on Personnel Studies in Special Education. Retrieved February 5, 2006 from *http://copsse.org/*.

Billingsley, B. S. (2004). Promoting teacher quality and retention in special education. [Electronic version]. *Journal of Learning Disabilities, 37,* 370–376.

Billingsley, B. S., Carlson, E., & Klein, S. (2004). The working conditions and induction support of early career special educators. [Electronic version]. *Exceptional Children, 70,* 333–347.

Brownell, M. (2000). Coping with stress in the special education classroom: Can individual teachers more effectively manage stress? Reston, VA: Eric Digest. [Eric Document Reproductive Service No. E545]

Brownell, M. T. (2005). The center on personnel studies in special education: Research issues in teacher education [Electronic version]. *The Journal of Special Education, 38,* 241.

Brownell, M. T., Hirsch, E., & Seo, S. (2004). Meeting the demand for highly qualified special education teachers during severe shortages: What should policymakers consider? [Electronic version]. *The Journal of Special Education, 38,* 56–61.

Brownell, M. T., Ross, D. D., Colon, E. P., & McCallum, C. L. (2005). Critical features of special education teacher preparation: A comparison with general education teacher education [Electronic version]. *The Journal of Special Education, 38,* 242–252.

Council for Exceptional Children (2004). Take this job and love it. *Today. 10*(5), pp. 1, 7, 17, 19.

Darling-Hammond, L. (2003). Keeping good teachers: Why it matters, what leaders can do. *Educational Leadership, 60*(8), 6–13.

Davis, M., Eshelman, E. R., & McKay, M. (2000). *The relaxation and stress reduction workbook.* Oakland, CA: New Harbinger Publications, Inc.

Futernick, K. (2007). A possible dream: Retaining California teachers so that all students learn. Sacramento: California State University.

Gersten, R., Keating, T., Yovanoff, P., & Karniss, M. K. (2001). Working in special education: Factors that enhance special educators' intent to stay. [Electronic version]. *Exceptional Children, 67,* 549–567.

Graziano, C. (2005). School's out. *Edutopia, 1*(3), 38–44.

Growing and improving the special education teacher workforce: A focus on beginning teachers can help. (2005, February). *Special Education Workforce Watch: Insights from Research,* pp. 1–2. Retrieved February 5, 2006 from *http://copsse.org.*

Holloway, J. J. (2001). The benefits of mentoring [Electronic version]. *Educational Leadership, 58,* 85–86.

Smith, H. W. (1994). *The ten natural laws of successful time and life management.* New York: Time Warner Books.

Weil, A. (1996) Eight Steps to Stress relief. *Self Healing Newsletter.* Marion, OH.

Whitaker, S. D. (2000). Mentoring beginning special education teachers and the relationship to attrition. *Exceptional Children, 66,* 546–566.

Whitaker, S. D. (2001). Supporting beginning special education teachers. [Electronic version]. *Focus on Exceptional Children, 34*(4), 1–18.

White, M., & Mason, C. (2003). Mentoring induction principles and guidelines (draft). Retrieved August 8, 2005 from *http://www.cec.sped.org/spotlight/udl/mip_g_manual_11pt.pdf.*

NAME INDEX

SUBJECT INDEX